MACHINE INTELLIGENCE

DEMYSTIFYING MACHINE LEARNING, NEURAL NETWORKS AND DEEP LEARNING

SURESH SAMUDRALA

INDIA • SINGAPORE • MALAYSIA

Notion Press

Old No. 38, New No. 6
McNichols Road, Chetpet
Chennai - 600 031

First Published by Notion Press 2018
Copyright © Suresh Samudrala 2018
All Rights Reserved.

ISBN 978-1-68466-082-7

Contents

Abstract

In the last few years, we are surrounded by systems enriched with machine learning and deep learning technologies. So far, adaptation is predominantly by large technology firms with deep research budgets. Significant progress has been made in consumer technology with quite encouraging results. Applications enriched with machine learning technologies reaching millions of users through smartphones is a reality today. Voice assistants, language translation, face recognition and AI enabled cameras are extensively in use today. Enterprises across different industries are keen to take advantage of these technologies and are investing in research and development in this space. In the enterprise world, we can see the early adaptation of machine learning techniques in areas like chatbots and voice assistants, processing user interactions in natural language. Enterprises are trying to catch up with the speed of innovation in these technologies to enhance enterprise value creation.

Machine learning technologies and techniques used to be predominantly the competence of scholars and research scientists. These algorithms are quite intense with loads of complex mathematical formulas, which can only be understood with an in-depth knowledge of linear algebra, probability and information theory. As machine learning discipline gains prominence and these technologies start moving from labs to enterprise data centers, there is a need to expand the skill base. Now that industries are looking to adopt these technologies on a large scale, the need for skilled professionals is continuously on the rise.

IT professionals across the industries are looking to up-skill in this area, as it is considered as one of the hot skills in the industry.

In today's world, the easiest thing to do in machine learning is coding as there are a number of tools and open source libraries available to develop solutions in this area. However, coding machine learning programs without an appreciation for the science behind it is like driving blindfolded. Lack of understanding of the concepts can be a big handicap in developing and configuring advanced machine learning based solutions.

Many IT professionals and students are quite interested to learn these concepts but are turned off by the complex mathematical formulas. That triggered my question: "Is it possible to explain machine learning concepts and algorithms without worrying about the complex mathematical formulas?"; "Is it possible to design and develop machine learning models without first understanding partial derivatives, eigenvectors and matrix operations?" This book is an attempt toward building fundamental knowledge in machine learning explained without mathematical formulas.

Mathematics is at the heart of machine learning but is a complex subject and requires practice and expertise. But every mathematical formula has an intuitive meaning which is much easier to understand. In this book, I have explained the intuitive meaning of popular machine learning algorithms without actually going into the formulas behind it. I have used the narrative style to describe the issues leading to the problem statement, how different algorithms address the problem and various design parameters. This book explains the core concepts of machine learning in plain English using illustrations, data tables and examples. Technology principles, design considerations and limitations have been explained without having to work out underlying mathematical formulas.

This book is intended for IT and business professionals from different industries looking to up-skill themselves in this emerging technology area.

This book can be used to get a good insight into underlying concepts in machine learning. This book is also useful for students in the area of artificial intelligence and machine learning to gain a conceptual understanding of the algorithms behind the mathematical formulas. Students can gain an industry perspective on these technologies, which would help them better prepare for a career in this field.

This book focuses on the fundamental concepts and algorithms which are timeless and avoids programming examples as these platforms are evolving rapidly. Technology platforms and libraries which can be used to experiment have been listed in the 'References and Resources' section. There are several sources for programming examples available in the public domain on the internet on all these platforms which readers can refer to.

Contents of this book are based on a sound understanding of the mathematical formulas and numerous experiments conducted on various models. However, I understand this is a vast area and am open to receive any feedback to improve or correct the contents of this book.

Foreword

The availability of computing and communication resources for collecting, storing and processing huge amounts of data has changed the way we gather user behaviour, develop business models, visualize applications and involve in research activities. The underlying tasks in these activities are being carried out through machine learning (ML) tools and techniques. *Machine learning* is an all-encompassing term involving processing the data to look for trends or patterns. These trends or patterns help in understanding the process that is generating the data. The process can then be used to predict the user behaviour and evolve suitable business models. Researchers attempt to develop methods to extract the patterns, derive the process, develop a prediction model and infer the outcome from sample data.

Since human beings seem to perform effortlessly the tasks of pattern processing and inferencing from sample data, even in changing environments, these tasks are attributed to *intelligence*. If these tasks are carried out by a machine, then they are attributed to *Artificial Intelligence* (AI) or machine intelligence. The tools and techniques that make AI happen constitute the scope of machine learning. The key idea in machine learning is that pattern processing, inferencing and adaptation capabilities are implicitly captured from the data. Machine learning addresses issues like learning associations, supervised learning as in classification and regression, unsupervised learning as in clustering, and reinforcement learning. These issues are addressed using algorithms based on statistical approaches, artificial neural network models and deep learning methods. The statistical approaches include regression, decision trees, Bayesian learning, support vector machines (SVM) and k-means method. The deep learning methods include convolutional neural networks (CNN), recurrent neural networks (RNN) and long short-term memory (LSTM).

This book deals with the above topics of machine learning in a descriptive manner, explaining the concepts behind the tools and techniques, using simple illustrations. The author presents an organization of machine learning algorithms based on the characteristics of the problem, input, algorithm, solution, output and explainability. The methodology and implementation issues are presented briefly in the chapter on machine learning overview. All the remaining chapters cover the machine learning techniques. In particular, the chapters cover the following topics: Data analysis and preprocessing, preprocessing of unstructured data like text and multimedia, parametric regression techniques, decision trees and forests, support vector machine, Bayesian learning, k-means clustering, neural networks and deep learning including CNN, RNN and LSTM.

The author provides software options available for implementation of the machine learning techniques. Some real-life applications and use cases are also provided to give a feel for the application of the material presented in this book.

On the whole, I consider this book to be an excellent introduction to topics on machine learning. This will definitely motivate an inquisitive reader to appreciate the paradigm shift taking place in data processing through machine learning, leading to applications of AI in practically every aspect of human activity.

I congratulate the author Suresh Samudrala for this great effort.

Prof. B Yegnanarayana,
FNAE, FNA, FASc, FIEEE, FISCA
INSA Senior Scientist
IIIT Hyderabad

Acknowledgments

I received positive and encouraging feedback on my earlier books on banking technology. This motivated me to pursue and focus my writings on most disruptive technologies. I would like to thank all my readers for their support. I am thankful to my family, friends and colleagues who have supported me in successfully completing this project.

I would like to thank Prof. B Yegnanarayana, IIIT Hyderabad for providing an excellent and insightful foreword. He has kindly accepted my request despite his busy schedule as the General Chair for a global conference on Speech Recognition – Interspeech 2018 held in Hyderabad. I am also thankful to him for his detailed review and feedback on the book.

I would like to thank Mr. Whee Teck ONG, CEO of Trusted Source and VP of Singapore Computer Society for reviewing my book and providing his positive views. I am also thankful to him for finding my previous book on banking technology relevant to be included in the reading list for a course on 'IT Mediated Financial Solutions and Platforms' in his previous role as a professor at National University of Singapore (NUS).

I would like to thank Mr. Siddhartha S, Founder and CEO of Intain, a financial technology startup focusing on AI and blockchain, for his support in reviewing the book and providing his positive views. He has taken time out to support this project despite his busy schedule in building the organization.

I would also like to thank Mr. Yagneswara Sarma Bulusu, for his time and efforts in supporting me in the reviews and finalizing the script.

Finally, I would like to thank my publishers Notion Press, for their support and professional work in this project.

1

Decoding the Jargon

1.1 Introduction

In any emerging technology, it is natural that a lot of jargon is used and many times interchangeably; artificial intelligence and machine learning are no different. There are a lot of terms like AI, machine learning, neural networks, Robotic Process Automation (RPA), supervised learning and deep learning used in the context of these technologies. In this chapter, we will look at a conceptual understanding of these terms.

Artificial Intelligence can be broadly defined as:

'Systems that can analyze, reason and act on real-world events and data similar to or better than humans.'

Going by this definition, we can consider every software that is ever written as intelligent. Existing IT systems, which are in operation for decades, perform amazing tasks with high accuracy which humans cannot even imagine matching. IT systems that process millions of payments and ensure the right beneficiary receiving funds are super intelligent. Stock exchange systems that match millions of orders between brokers are definitely intelligent. ATM machines have the intelligence to verify the customer's identity and count/dispense the exact cash to customers in a more cost-efficient manner than a human teller.

We have intelligent systems in various industries/areas like government, healthcare and retail that perform amazing things to ensure that a customer is serviced efficiently and at the lowest cost possible. Can anyone deny the intelligence of these IT systems that have been in use for several decades? If we have already had intelligent systems for decades, what is the buzz about artificial intelligence now?

Figure 1 gives an overview of the various terms used and how they are related.

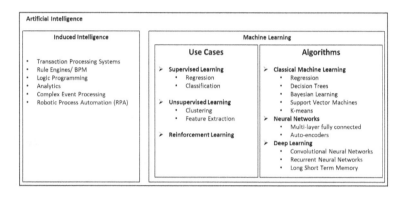

Figure 1. Artificial Intelligence and Machine Learning Jargon

At the highest level, we can take it that every system is intelligent. As we have seen in the examples, existing systems perform better than humans in terms of speed and accuracy and hence the entire universe of IT systems is presented as artificially intelligent in figure 1. However, we break down the universe of intelligent systems into 2 broad categories:

Induced Intelligence: Intelligence is the ability to analyze, reason and act on real-world events. This requires knowledge and intelligence about the business rules, validations and processing calendar/timelines. In traditional IT systems, this intelligence is induced into them in various forms. Typically, programmers understand the validations and business rules to capture them in machine-readable language to build IT systems. This knowledge is extracted from the business users and fed into the systems by IT teams. Differences in the knowledge between what the user has in mind and what is coded into IT systems result in a defect. Users talk in a different language than what IT systems can understand, and this results in such defects.

Evolution of software engineering has a single purpose: to reduce the transmission loss of knowledge flowing from business subject matter experts (SMEs) to IT systems through a bunch of programmers. Rules engines are built to externalize business rules from the IT systems to give the control of maintaining the intelligence into the hands of business SMEs. Similarly, agile methodologies ensure that there is an efficient flow of knowledge between business and IT teams with shorter feedback cycles to validate the captured intelligence.

Figure 2 captures the induced intelligence life cycle.

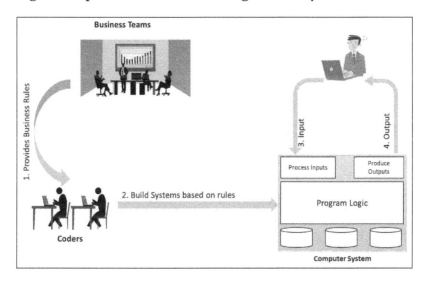

Figure 2. Induced Intelligence

- Step 1: Business specifies the requirements in terms of logic/ rules.

- Step 2: Coders build the logic into the system either programmatically or using tools.

- Step 3: Inputs are received by the system and processed according to the rules.

- Step 4: Outputs/decisions are produced by the system.

Robotic Process Automation (RPA), which is commonly bucketed under artificial intelligence, is a case of induced intelligence. Using RPA tools, manual user actions are mimicked by IT systems. RPA is typically used in less frequently occurring manual actions, which do not justify a business case for full-fledged automation.

Machine Learning: Machine learning is a set of tools and techniques, in which intelligence is learned by algorithms and not induced. These systems analyze historical data patterns to extract intelligence and convert them into business rules. We have already seen that IT systems with induced intelligence perform amazing things and constitute a major part of technology in the world today. Then why bother with machine learning?

There are mainly 2 areas in which machine learning can provide an edge:

- In induced intelligence, knowledge comes from business users/ SMEs. But how do they get this knowledge? Business SMEs develop an intuitive understanding of the relationships between various events and business outcomes by analyzing past business scenarios and results. For example, business SMEs arrive at the criteria for approving a mortgage to an employed individual based on the historical learning of the bank as well as collective knowledge of the industry. Similarly, rules for identifying a fraudulent payment transaction is arrived at and continuously updated by business SMEs based on their observation of the past data and learnings. Business SME knowledge is rare and expensive. Also, humans have limited capability when analyzing and summarizing insights from a large number of data elements. It is possible to miss some of the changes happening in the industry as they tend to gain insights only from a few key parameters. What if we are able to extract the intelligence from the data automatically? What if we are able to revise the business rules whenever we notice a change in the data patterns? Machine learning can really help here.

- For induced intelligence, we need the rules to be explicitly specified by the business so that IT teams can capture them into the systems. What about problems for which solutions cannot be described in the form of rules? We all know how to identify a face in an image but cannot specify how we do it in the form of rules. To prove this, try specifying rules for identifying a face in an image. Similarly, we cannot specify rules for identifying handwritten text or analyzing videos. We humans have cognitive skills which make it easy for even a small child to perform these tasks effortlessly. Machine learning techniques can help in teaching systems how to perform cognitive functions such as vision, speech and natural language text.

In summary, machine learning can help us generate patterns from much larger historical data than what business SMEs can process. It can help us understand the changing patterns in data by learning from recent data. Machine learning can also provide a cognitive capability which cannot be specified in the form rules to be captured using induced intelligence.

Figure 3 captures the machine learning life cycle.

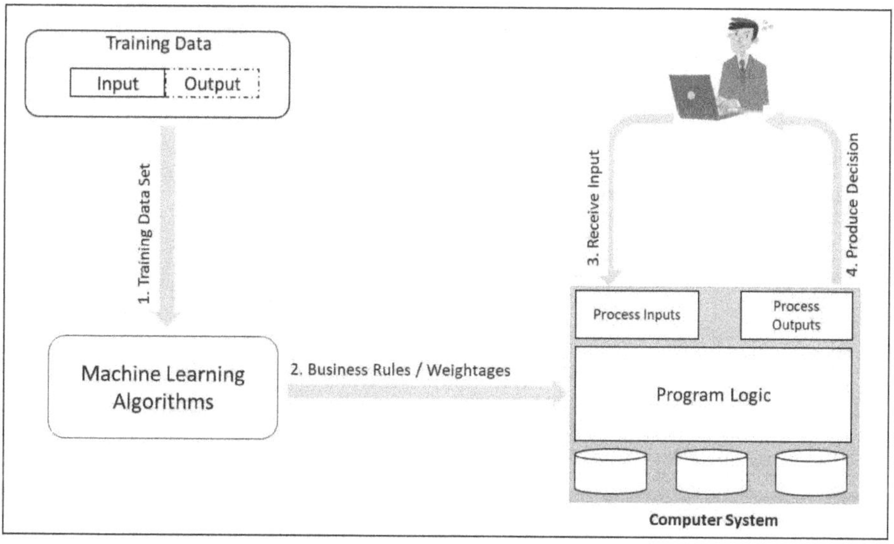

Figure 3. Intelligence Learned by Machines

- Step 1: Training dataset is given as input to machine learning algorithm.

- Step 2: Machine learning algorithm arrives at the processing rules.

- Step 3: Inputs are received and processed according to the rules computed by machine learning algorithm.

- Step 4: Output/decision is produced.

Rest of the book focuses on the right-hand side box titled 'Machine Learning' in figure 1.

1.2   Key Terms

In the rest of the book, we will use some key terms related to machine learning technology. These terms are used interchangeably in the industry and hence a quick mapping is presented in the below table.

Jargon	Description
Feature Variable Independent Variable Input Variable	These terms represent the input variables in the historical training data.
Label Variable Dependent Variable Output Variable	These terms represent the output variable of the machine learning model.
Parameters Weights Bias Weight Matrix User Induced Variables	These terms refer to the variables in the machine learning model that are modified during the training process to capture the knowledge from the training data.

Prediction Inference Output	These terms refer to the process of using the trained model to produce output for unseen records.
Training Data Historical Data Historical Training Data	These terms refer to the data available to build and train the model.
Neural Networks Artificial Neural Networks	These terms refer to a class of machine learning algorithms.

1.3 Classification of Machine Learning Algorithms

Compared to human intelligence, machine learning is still very nascent and localized to the problem for which it is designed. We do not have systems that observe events happening in multiple disciplines and gain intelligence from them. Machine learning algorithms are able to learn only those specific things for which they are designed and trained. Machine learning algorithms are very much use case specific and are under the control of human engineers who design them. There is a separate research going on in the space of Artificial General Intelligence (AGI) which is about human-like intelligence with machines that can set their own agenda and make their own decisions. AGI is outside the scope of this book.

At the crux of it, machine learning is about finding the interdependencies/relationships between data. All the machine learning algorithms mentioned in figure 1 have one single purpose: to extract the relationship between data elements. Once we have such a relationship established, it is easy for us to estimate future outcomes. To understand machine learning deeper, we need to be able to think in terms of relationships between data elements.

Machine learning algorithms can be classified in multiple ways depending on the nature of the problem, type of input and type of output. Let us look at some of the important ways machine learning algorithms are classified.

Classification Based on Nature of the Problem: Machine learning algorithms can be classified based on the nature of the problem that they are trying to solve.

> **Regression:** Variables that can take any numerical value are called continuous variables. The temperature of a city can take any value ranging from –50 to 50 degrees Celsius, the age of a person can range from 0 to 120 and the marks of a student can range from 0 to 100. Machine learning algorithms developed to predict such variables are called regression algorithms. Regression algorithms capture the relation between various input variables and the output variable to build a predictive model. Regression model for predicting the marks of a student can take various inputs like number of study hours, parent's profession, parent's qualification, school and other similar parameters.

> **Classification:** Variables that can take one of the possible values from a predefined list are called categorical variables. The grade of a student can be 'A,' 'B' or 'C' or a company's rating can be 'AAA,' 'AA' or 'BBB'; these are examples of categorical variables. Classification algorithms predict the possible category of the output given a set of input variables. Sometimes, a given problem can be structured as either regression or classification use case. Student grade prediction algorithm is a classification use case whereas predicting the exact marks is a regression use case.

> **Clustering:** The ability to group the given data records into a specified number of cohesive units is called clustering. A retail store may want to cluster its clients into a few groups and target the customers with high potential with special offers. Clustering algorithm looks at the given set of input variables like average number of visits, number of purchases and purchase value and group them into a given number of clusters. Unlike regression or classification, we do not specify the historical output as part of training. The algorithm finds the most suitable grouping of records based on the training data.

Classification Based on Nature of Inputs: Machine learning algorithms are also classified based on the nature of inputs required by the algorithm at the time of training.

> **Supervised Learning:** Machine learning algorithms that require historical input as well as corresponding output are called supervised learning techniques. It is referred to as 'supervised' because we are providing the historical output apart from input features. The regression and classification algorithms discussed above are typical examples of supervised learning techniques.

> **Unsupervised Learning:** These algorithms do not require us to specify the historical output. Clustering algorithms are an example of an unsupervised algorithm. Unsupervised algorithms are also used for feature extraction from historical data and then to use the features to train a supervised learning algorithm like regression or classification.

> **Reinforcement Learning:** Supervised learning algorithms require training data to be presented in the form pairs of input and output records. Reinforcement algorithm works as an agent in an environment with several possible actions to choose from. The agent selects the best action from the possible ones in the given environment state. The agent receives risk/reward inputs from the environment based on the selected action. The algorithm learns by optimizing the agent's actions to increase the reward and reduce the risk. As the learning happens over several time steps, the algorithm learns to balance between short-term risks vs. long-term rewards to maximize overall score.

Once trained, the algorithm can predict the next best possible move for a given state to optimize the reward. Video games are a good example; they provide different game states at any point for the agent to act on. Each action in the form of game moves by the agent is rewarded with a positive score or punished with a penalty. Trained model optimizes the game moves in such a way that the overall score is maximized.

Classification Based on Nature of the Algorithm: Machine learning algorithms are broadly classified into 3 categories based on the nature of the algorithm.

Classical Machine Learning: These algorithms, which are also called statistical machine learning, use mathematical and statistical equations to derive the relationships in the training data. Classical machine learning techniques come with the advantage of explain-ability which is very important for certain use cases. This is the capability to explain the reason for the given prediction for the given input data. The following statistical machine learning techniques are discussed in detail in this book:

- Decision Trees, Random Forests

- Bayesian Learning, Naive Bayes

- Support Vector Machines

- K-Means Clustering

Neural Networks: Neural networks are inspired by the human brain and the way it learns. As the human brain learns a skill, new connections are established between neurons in the brain. Similarly, in neural networks, complex mathematical models with a large number of trainable parameters are built. These parameters are trained based on the training data to build the model. As the trained mathematical model captures the complex relationships in the training datasets, it can be used for future predictions as well. We will discuss neural networks and their key design issues in 2 dedicated chapters. Neural networks hold a lot of promise but have limitations in learning when the complexity of the model increases. Neural networks also have limitations in capturing complex dependencies like spatial/temporal relationships.

Deep Learning: Deep learning algorithms are based on the underlying principles of neural networks but have advanced architecture to cater to their limitations. Key architecture principles and design issues of deep learning are similar to neural networks. However, deep learning algorithms have special features to cater to learning spatial/temporal relationships, which are useful in problems like machine vision and natural language processing. Deep learning algorithms also address the issues of limited learning prevalent in neural networks. We will look at the following deep learning algorithms in dedicated chapters for each of them:

- Convolutional Neural Networks

- Recurrent Neural Networks

- Long Short-Term Memory

Classification Based on the Solution: At its core, machine learning is about extracting insights from historical training data. In supervised learning use cases, we have historical data records in the form of input and output pairs. Once trained, the algorithm is expected to predict the output for any future inputs. So, our solution can take one of the following approaches:

Parametric Models: In parametric models, our prediction output depends only on the future inputs. Here, we establish a relationship between historical inputs and corresponding outputs and expect that the same is maintained for any unseen future records. In such an approach, each of the inputs is given a weightage parameter depending on their influence on the output. So, our prediction is based only on the values of the future inputs. These models are called parametric models as the solution consists of a weightage parameter for each input, indicating the level of influence on the prediction. Linear regression techniques and neural networks are some of the examples of parametric models.

Non-Parametric Models: Our prediction output depends not only on the future input values but also on previous outputs.

In this approach, the value of the prediction output is derived from the values of the output in similar circumstances earlier identified from training data. The non-parametric model tries to identify the closest historical data record or group of records and produces their average output as a prediction. In this model, there are no parameters weighing the inputs to arrive at the prediction and hence are called non-parametric models. Decision trees and nearest neighbors algorithms are examples of this category.

Training the parametric and non-parametric models requires completely different approaches. Training parametric models requires us to use linear algebra and derivatives to find the optimum parameters that fit the historical training data. Parameters (also called as weights) are specified for each feature in the input data, representing the importance of that feature on the output. The algorithm computes the parameters in such a way that for the historical input, the model produces the output which is closest to the given output.

On the other hand, training the non-parametric model is about optimally grouping the training data into buckets, with each bucket representing a valid group of records from training data. As part of the prediction for a new record, the closest bucket is identified and the average of output from the training records in that bucket is taken as the prediction. Here, training is based on statistics and information theory to be able to arrive at the best possible grouping of the training data. Decision trees split the training data into different buckets at the leaf node along with the hierarchy of decision criteria to put any new records into a given bucket. Similarly, the nearest neighbors algorithm computes the prediction by choosing the average across training records which are closer to the given record in multi-dimensional space.

Classification Based on the Nature of Output: Inferences generated by machine learning algorithms are abstract. Two models trained on the same data can have different inferences in certain cases. This is different from rule-based systems in which output is always fixed. We can classify the models based on whether they give a measure of the quality of the prediction apart from the prediction itself.

Probabilistic Models: Probabilistic machine learning models give the estimated probability of the prediction as a measure of confidence. For example, knowing that a particular transaction is 80% likely to be fraudulent is more useful than just marking it as fraudulent or not. Probabilities are relevant for classification use cases as each possible category of label can be assigned a probability by the model. Some machine learning models are inherently probabilistic. We will see in the later chapters that naive Bayes algorithm computes the probabilities for each category of output label to arrive at the prediction. Similarly, neural networks with the softmax function at the output layer also produce probability distribution for all output categories.

Non-probabilistic Models: These models provide the prediction, but they do not provide any information on the quality of prediction. Machine learning models like decision trees and support vector machines (SVM) are inherently non-probabilistic in their predictions. In certain cases, it might be important to get the measure of confidence on the prediction. Ensemble techniques can provide a measure of confidence on the prediction. The idea behind the ensemble technique is to develop multiple machine learning algorithms for the given problem and aggregate the prediction based on certain rules. Prediction made by a maximum number of models can be taken as the prediction of the ensemble. Ensemble methods provide the probability/level of confidence on the output classes even if the underlying machine learning algorithms are not probabilistic. Ensemble techniques also help in generalizing the solution by removing model bias.

Classification Based on Explain-ability: One of the key concerns related to machine learning algorithms is the explain-ability. The rationale for decisions taken by traditional IT systems with induced intelligence can be explained by the rules captured in the system. A particular transaction is considered fraudulent because its value is 10 times the previous maximum transaction by the customer; this can be a valid explanation. The capability of the machine learning algorithm to provide traceability to the decision is called 'explain-ability.' Certain machine learning algorithms have better explain-ability than others and some algorithms simply produce the prediction without any explanation. Statistical learning techniques like decision trees and naive Bayes have better capability to explain than neural networks. Deep learning algorithms like convolutional neural networks (CNN) or LSTM have near zero capability to explain the decisions.

We may not need an explanation for all machine learning predictions. For all decision support use cases where machine learning prediction is used for decisions like validating a transaction or approving a loan, it is important to know the rationale considering transparency and regulatory perspectives. However, cognitive use cases like image classification and voice sentiment will not require the algorithm to have the capability to explain. We have seen that these are the use cases in which humans are not able to explain the rules, so we cannot expect the algorithms to do the same. We may not need to know how the algorithm identified a face in the image or captured the sentiment in the voice as we ourselves are not able to describe it in the first place. The capability of the algorithm to provide explanation can be an important factor in choosing the algorithm if the use cases require it.

1.4 Ensemble Approach

Finding the right machine learning model with optimally tuned parameters is to some extent based on trial and error. Induced intelligence-based systems give an exact decision as their output is based on coded rules. However, the output from machine learning algorithms is abstract. Depending on the training data, training sequence and model, the predicted output can vary. However, we need to know how accurate our algorithm's predictions are. There are no mathematical formulas to choose the right model and model parameters to arrive at the optimal results directly. Ensemble approach is used to address this problem.

In the ensemble approach, several machine learning models are built and trained for the given problem. These models generate predictions independently, which are then aggregated to arrive at the final prediction. Aggregation of the predictions from each of the models in the ensemble ensures that any bias built into any model for the given record does not impact the result.

Ensemble models generalize the predictions better and also provide us with the probability or confidence score. We can infer the confidence level on the output depending on the number of models predicting the same result. Assuming that we have built 5 models to predict whether a customer loan can be approved, then each model gives an independent prediction. In this case, we have the probability of the loan being repaid as 80% if 4 of the 5 models predict the 'Loan Eligibility' as 'Yes.' Figure 4 depicts an ensemble approach to machine learning predictions.

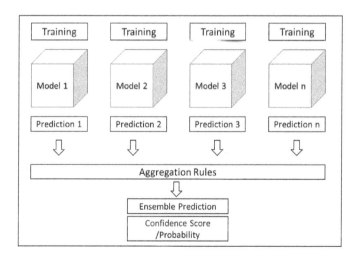

Figure 4. Ensemble-Based Machine Learning Approach

We will have a detailed look at the machine learning algorithms in the rest of the book. We will cover statistical machine learning, neural networks and deep learning algorithms, in that order, in dedicated chapters for each algorithm.

2

Machine Learning Overview

We humans create mental models to understand complex real-world scenarios and react to various external world events based on these models engraved in our brains. Machine learning is about creating a model that closely represents that part of the real world which is captured in the training data. Machine learning models consist of mathematical formulas, decision criteria and multi-dimensional parameters. In this chapter, we will look at use cases, project methodology and other fundamental concepts related to machine learning algorithms.

2.1 Types of Use Cases

In the earlier chapter, we discussed that the majority of the IT systems today have induced intelligence and 2 scenarios in which machine learning capabilities could complement induced intelligence.

- Ability to generate insights from large volumes of structured data in a systematic manner. Human experts are only able to analyze a limited quantity of data and can get carried away by emotions.

- Ability to solve the problems which cannot be specified as rules. For example, identifying a face in an image or understanding the sentiment of a text message or speech, etc. These tasks are effortlessly done by humans but cannot be explained in the form of rules.

Based on the above description, we can classify machine learning use cases into 2 categories:

- Decision support use cases

- Cognitive use cases

Decision Support Use Cases: Decision support use cases generate insights from large volumes of structured data to augment or even replace the decision rules set up by experts. For example, identifying a fraudulent card transaction is traditionally done using a set of rules captured in the transaction authentication system. These rules are defined by business experts based on their experience of noticing such transactions. However, we can augment/replace such a rule engine with a prediction engine built on machine learning models. Machine learning model trained on a large historical dataset of valid and fraudulent transactions can predict whether a given new transaction is genuine or fraudulent. Some more examples of use cases in this category:

- Predicting whether a customer will be able to repay the loan.

- Predicting the probability of a customer/employee leaving the organization.

- Forecasting the sales of a product during the festive season.

- Forecasting the future movements in the stock market.

Cognitive Use Cases: These use cases perform human-like cognitive tasks in the areas of natural language processing, speech, image and vision. These problems are hard to solve using induced intelligence as the rules could not be specified clearly. These problems can be addressed better by using machine learning. Algorithms for cognitive use cases are rapidly evolving with a step change in the performance of these algorithms in the last few years. Deep learning algorithms, which we will discuss later in the book, have been the foundation of that breakthrough. Some of the examples for use cases in this category:

- Language translation

- Text classification

- Speech recognition

- Image recognition

As you can see from the above examples, decision support use cases predominantly work with structured data as input whereas cognitive use cases work with unstructured data. Machine learning algorithms always expect numerical variables as input, irrespective of the use case. So, it is up to the developers to prepare the numerical input to the algorithm from structured or unstructured data. For deciding whether a particular loan can be issued, we may feed in a number of data points like employment status, existing loans, loan-to-income ratio and number of dependents. These data points are presented as continuous or categorical variables to the algorithm. Similarly, for identifying a face in an image, we may feed in the density of each pixel in the image as a continuous variable.

For natural language processing, we represent the text in the form of numbers using text representation techniques. So, from a machine learning algorithm perspective, it does not differentiate between structured and unstructured data. The algorithm always receives inputs as numerical values to compute dependencies between different inputs and outputs.

2.2 Project Methodology

Every IT project has a life cycle of its own. Building a customer-facing mobile app requires significant focus on user experience and ease of use. Development of transaction processing engine requires detailed capturing of processing, validation and computation rules. For the success of any IT project, there needs to be a significant coordination between business and technology teams. In machine learning programs, there is an even thinner line between business and technology. Fundamentally, machine learning programs are sophisticated trial and error methods. So, it is imperative that a multi-disciplinary team contributes to the program from concept to the implementation stage. It is also necessary to review the effectiveness of the implemented solution at regular intervals and retrain the models as necessary.

Let us look at the typical life cycle of a machine learning program.

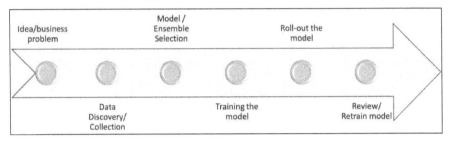

Figure 5. Machine Learning Methodology

Idea/Business Problem: A key driver for a machine learning program is an idea or a business problem which can be addressed by a machine learning algorithm. This can be about predicting the customer churn or finding customer sentiment from social media or eliminating the fraud or even generating insights from satellite imagery.

Data Discovery/Collection: It is the most crucial step of the program and can largely decide the outcome. Data discovery is the process of identifying internal as well as external data sources which can help in addressing the problem. As we are extracting intelligence from data, the focus should be on identifying and collecting data from innovative sources apart from the traditional ones. Additional data sources help models develop competitive advantage compared to systems taking decisions purely based on traditional data sources.

Model/Ensemble Section: Selection of model or ensemble of models depends on various factors such as:

- Nature of the problem (Regression, Classification, Clustering, etc.)

- Number of data records available for training

- Decision support or cognitive use case?

- Need for explain-ability

Algorithm choice and data preparation vary for regression and classification problems. In many cases, a given problem can be structured as a regression or classification problem. For example, prediction of 1-week future market price can be defined as a classification problem as shown below.

- Class 1 – Market price rises by > 10%

- Class 2 – Market price changes between –10% and 10%

- Class 3 – Market price falls by >10%

The same problem can be specified as a regression problem by predicting the % of change in the market price or even predicting the absolute price. It is important to structure the problem in such a way that it is better predictable. For example, regressing a % change in the stock price gives better predictability than an absolute value as the absolute value changes over the training time period.

Number of data records available can also influence the choice of the machine learning algorithm. Machine learning algorithms like support vector machines (SVM) can work with fewer training records whereas neural networks and deep learning algorithms require large amounts of data to be able to train the model effectively.

Nature of use case can be a factor in determining the machine learning algorithm. Decision support related use cases can be achieved by both statistical learning techniques as well as neural networks-based models. For example, identification of non-performing loans or fraudulent transactions can be done using either statistical learning methods (like random forest, Bayesian learning, etc.) or neural networks-based prediction engines. For use cases that involve speech, image, natural language and video recognition, deep learning algorithms like convolutional networks or LSTM are better suited to find an optimal solution.

Certain use cases require explain-ability, which means that there needs to be traceability between the decisions and the supplied input. This is mainly relevant in decision support related use cases and not so much for cognitive use cases. For use cases that require explain-ability, statistical learning models are better suited as neural networks-based models do not provide a good explanation of the prediction.

Training the Model: Following aspects need to be considered for training the models.

For training the model, historical data needs to be segregated into 3 parts:

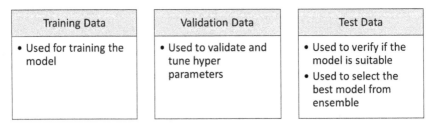

Training Data	Validation Data	Test Data
• Used for training the model	• Used to validate and tune hyper parameters	• Used to verify if the model is suitable • Used to select the best model from ensemble

Figure 6. Training Data Components

Training Data: Typically, 60–70% of the historical data is marked as training data. Training data is used to build the machine learning model. This can be for building the decision tree or computing the support vectors or computing the weights in a neural network or combination of all in an ensemble. Training accuracy is a measure of prediction accuracy of the model on training data.

Validation Data: Typically, 20–30% of the historical data is marked as validation data. Each machine learning algorithm has several hyperparameters which control the nature of the learning. For example, the learning rate in neural networks specifies the amount of incremental change to the parameters in every learning iteration. Training data is used to build the model for a particular combination of hyperparameters. Validation data is used to measure the accuracy of the trained model and tune the hyperparameters to improve the learning if needed.

Test Data: Typically, 10–20% of the data is marked as test data. It is always recommended to mark the test data and segregate it first. Test data is the last test for the model after all iterations of training and tuning are over. Data seen by the model during training and tuning phases can be assumed to be built into the model. Hence, test data should be left as the 'true test' of the model's performance.

There are different approaches to splitting the data.

– Historical records are randomly split into 3 buckets for training, validation and testing.

– Several combinations of training and validation records can be generated from the same dataset. In this approach, the model can be tested with different training datasets and verified with the corresponding validation dataset. Average error/accuracy across these models gives us a good indication of the performance of the model

– Split the historical data in such a way that all 3 datasets have equal representation of output categories

The entire training process has been depicted in the figure 7:

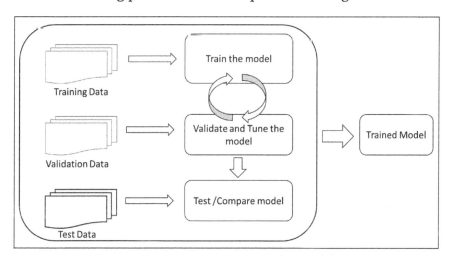

Figure 7. Training the Machine Learning Model

Train the Model: In this phase, the machine learning model is built in such a way that the computed result closely matches with the historical results for the training data.

Validate and Tune the Model: There are a number of parameters in the machine learning model which impact the learning but are not modified as part of training. For example, the learning rate parameter influences the amount of learning in each step. These parameters are called hyperparameters. Validation data is used to verify the trained model accuracy and make adjustments to hyperparameters to achieve the desired level of accuracy. We can consider that the validation data is also seen by the model as this data is used to set hyperparameters.

Testing Mode: In this phase, the model is tested using completely unseen data for which historical results are already available. Predicted results from the model are compared with the historical results to assess the correctness of the model. The model can be taken up for implementation only if the test results are satisfactory.

Rollout the Model: As discussed earlier, prediction from a trained model is a lot less resource intensive when compared to training. A trained model can be integrated into a user interface, mobile app or API for predictions based on future inputs.

Review/Retrain: There are many reasons for which the deployed model needs to be reviewed/retrained to keep it up-to-date.

- As the model is deployed for generating predictions on new records, there is a need to include the new data to refine the training. For example, in a stock index prediction model, several hundreds of thousands of new data records get created every day. It is only reasonable to retrain the model on a weekly/monthly basis to ensure that recent trends in data are built into the model.

- Learning from mistakes: For solutions like spam filters, movie recommendations and language translations, there is a continuous feedback on whether the given inference is correct or not based on user action. It is necessary to include such records back into the training so that future occurrence can be avoided.

- New datasets: For decision support use cases, prediction using the same datasets over a period of time by multiple parties will have diminishing returns. So, there is a need to continuously look for alternate data sources and datasets that can strengthen the models and the predictions.

It is imperative that there is continuous interaction between various business and technology stakeholders throughout the life cycle of the machine learning program.

2.3 Evaluating a Machine Learning Model

How do we evaluate if the trained model is reliable? Can we quantify the correctness of the model? Model evaluation depends on whether it is a regression or classification solution.

Regression Models: Prediction of a machine learning model and its accuracy are not absolute but should be in comparison with default accuracy. Default accuracy can be seen as the accuracy of the prediction made without spending any effort in building the model. Machine learning model predicting student marks with 80% accuracy may appear very good, but it actually depends on the historical data.

Let us say we have historical student data with marks ranging from 70 to 80 with an average of 75. Without building any model, using the average value of 75 as the prediction results in an error less than 5 for any training record. For this training data, the model performance of 80% accuracy looks poor as the baseline accuracy is better than the model performance. In this case, the model performed worse than the default accuracy and hence is completely useless.

In regression problems, the average (also called as mean) of all the historical outputs acts as the default prediction. In such an approach, the output of each record deviates from the average, resulting in an error for each record. The actual output deviates from the average due to the influence of certain parameters captured as features in the training data. These features influence the output for each record to go above or below the average. For example, higher study hours may push the student marks above the average whereas poor standards of the school may push the marks below the average. Regression algorithm should do better than such default error for it to be of any use. Regression algorithm needs to find the features that cause the output to deviate from average performance and should predict closer results.

R-squared is a measure of how well the regression algorithm is able to explain the deviations of the records from the mean. R-squared is the quantitative measure of the regression model performance against baseline performance. R-squared value of 1 indicates that the regression algorithm predicts the outcome accurately.

Classification Models: Classification models predict the category of output for the data records. A simple measure of classification models is the accuracy. A number of records correctly predicted by the machine learning model out of the total predictions are a measure of the accuracy of the model. However, it is also important to validate if the accuracy is uniformly distributed across output categories. Confusion matrix provides a view of the accuracy of the model across categories. Discrepancies in the accuracy across categories need to be analyzed even if overall accuracy looks high. Table 1 captures a sample confusion matrix.

Table 1. Confusion Matrix

Predicted Category/Actual Category	Category 1	Category 2	Category n
Category 1	95	3%	2%
Category 2	30%	50%	20%
Category n	5%	5%	90%

In the above table, the highlighted diagonal columns represent the correct categorization of the model. It can be noticed that the accuracy for category 2 is much less than the other categories. This may require further analysis of features and the model.

3

Data Analysis and Pre-Processing

We make decisions all the time in our individual capacity or in the executive role of an organization. We may or may not be using any structured methodology for decision making every time, but our minds intuitively go through analyzing all the information available to arrive at a decision. Let us look at some critical decisions that impact businesses:

- How much should I stuff my store for holiday season sale?

- Will this customer honor the loan repayment?

- Should we invest in a new plant and expand the capacity?

- How many people should I recruit next year?

- What will be the projected sales for my new product?

The soundness of our decision depends on how experienced we are in that field and if ever we faced similar situations in the past. People who have gained experience in a particular field over a long period of time are usually referred to as specialists as they may have insights into diverse scenarios and understand their implications to take a decision. For important decisions, understanding similar incidents in the past plays a significant role in identifying any flaws. We rely on specialists to derive such insights to predict the most likely future to arrive at decisions. Predictions of specialists are based on their experiences and hence things may not always develop the way they predicted. Specialists are also humans; their ability to process data is limited and they are also prone to emotions and hype.

Historical data holds valuable insights provided we have techniques and algorithms to extract those insights. It requires large amounts of diverse datasets to be able to extract such deep insights. Specialists may have an intuitive understanding of the interrelationships between the data whereas algorithms provide the capability to crunch large amounts of data without any bias/emotions. A combination of strong domain knowledge and advanced machine learning algorithms that generate actionable insights and intelligence can be a significant competitive advantage for any organization.

Data is at the core of the machine learning algorithms. As we have seen earlier, ML algorithms always take structured numerical data, either continuous or categorical, as the input. Analyzing, engineering and pre-processing the dataset to make it ready for ML algorithms is a significant part of any machine learning program.

Data analysis and processing can be broadly classified into 2 categories:

Structured Data for insights and decision support: In this category of use cases, we need to analyze large amounts of data to be able to provide actionable insights into a business. It requires a significant amount of effort in understanding the data and interrelationships as well as pre-processing of data before feeding it to a machine learning model. Business knowledge provides inputs on potential interrelationships between data attributes, which can be validated through data analysis. Also, data need to be pre-processed and normalized for effective use as part of the machine learning model.

Unstructured Data for cognitive use cases: Cognitive use cases like speech recognition, language translation, image recognition and video processing require the raw data to be processed and presented to the machine learning model for effective learning. Unlike data insights use cases, there is very little analysis of the data needed here, but a significant amount of pre-processing effort is needed to represent the data to the algorithm. Classical machine learning algorithms require key features from the unstructured data to be extracted manually and presented to the model for learning. These algorithms also have low accuracy. However, deep learning algorithms have the ability to extract the needed features from unstructured data like images and arrive at the needed inference.

As deep learning algorithms like CNN extract the needed features from images for learning, the amount of pre-processing needed is limited to converting raw data into a form that is readable by the machine learning model. Several techniques are used to represent natural language text to a machine learning model, depending on the use case. These representations can be in the form of bag-of-words, a sparse vector with each value representing a word in the model dictionary, or a dense vector created by using embedding techniques. Text documents need to be pre-processed using one of these techniques before being processed by machine learning models. In this chapter, we will discuss analyzing and pre-processing of structured data to prepare it for better learning by the machine learning models. Pre-processing of unstructured data like text and images is explained in the next chapter.

The importance of data cannot be overemphasized for machine learning. High quality and high-volume data can achieve greater results even with simple algorithms. However, it is also more expensive and difficult to get such data for a given problem statement. Let's look at some of the data considerations:

- **High Volume:** High volume of data ensures that we are learning and validating our model with more records and hence there is a higher probability of our prediction being right. There are techniques to generate additional records based on the original data for certain types of datasets. For example, image datasets can be skewed slightly to generate more data records.

- **Right Data:** Significant amount of time needs to be spent on feature engineering to ensure we are selecting the right attributes and presenting them in the right manner to the model for learning.

Knowledge of the domain and statistical analysis of the historical data are important elements to get this right. Domain knowledge will help us in identifying the right attributes and their presentation whereas statistical analysis will present us with additional insights in designing the solution.

- **Right Variety**: We need to ensure that the training data covers a wide range of scenarios and not disproportionately skewed for one category. This ensures that the network is generalized to ensure higher accuracy of future inferences.

Data analysis is a combination of the following themes:

Univariate Analysis: Analyzing each and every variable in the available data on a standalone basis. This gives us insight into the nature of data, its importance and how to pre-process it if it is found relevant.

Multivariate Analysis: Analyzing the interdependencies between the variables. Interdependencies between output variable (also called label or dependent variable) and each input variable (also called as feature variables or independent variables) provide the level of correlation between them and help us to choose the most important feature variables for the model. Analysis of correlation between the feature variables helps us eliminate highly correlated inputs to the model. Machine learning models generally perform better when there is little or no correlation between feature variables.

3.1 Univariate Analysis

Univariate analysis is about looking at and analyzing the feature and label variables in the training dataset separately with an aim to prepare the data for model training. The first thing to verify for each variable is the type of the data.

Types of Data: Based on the contents of the data in a variable, it can be categorized as one of the following types:

Numerical Continuous Data: Numerical continuous data can hold integer or decimal values. It can take any numerical value within a range. Some examples:

- Stock price ranges from 424 to 972

- Student mark ranges from 45 to 89

- Temperature in the city ranges from 21.4 to 34.5 units

Categorical Data: Variable contains one of the possible values from the list. Categorical data can be numeric or a set of character codes. Some examples:

- Car type ('Luxury,' 'Sedan,' 'Hatchback')

- Student grades ('A,' 'B,' 'C,' 'D')

- Transaction types (101, 201, 301, 401)

Date: These variables contain a date describing the record like issue date, expiry date and sale date. Date values cannot be used as is in the machine learning models. Date values need to be converted into a continuous variable or a categorical variable before it can be fed to a machine learning algorithm. For example:

- Date of construction of the house can be converted into age of the house in months.

- Date of birth can be used to create a categorical value ('teen,' 'young,' 'senior').

Domain knowledge and choice of the model influence the most appropriate way to convert a date column into a useful feature.

Distribution Analysis: Statistical summary of a numerical continuous data helps us understand the distribution.

Minimum, Maximum, Mean (Average): Minimum, maximum and average values of a continuous variable give us a good impression on the dataset and how the data is distributed. For example, age column in a customer dataset with the minimum age as 16, maximum age as 45 and average as 21 is already a lot of information. It indicates that the product range is attracting younger customers.

Standard Deviation and Variance: We computed the mean value in the previous step, which is a simple average of all the records. However, each record may have a value higher or lower than the mean value. Standard deviation is a measure of aggregate dispersion of data from the mean for all the records. A higher standard deviation is a measure of wide dispersion of data from the mean, whereas low standard deviation indicates that the given variable values are concentrated around mean values. Variance is a similar measure but has a higher scale as it is the square of the standard deviation.

In a class with an average score of 75, some students score above 75, some below 75 and a few way above or way below 75. The standard deviation is zero if all students score exactly 75; it results in the mean value of 75. However, the standard deviation is very high if 75% of the students score 100 and 25% of the students score zero, resulting in a class average of 75.

Histogram Analysis: Histogram analysis for categorical variables helps us understand the distribution. As mentioned earlier, categorical variables take one of the possible category values. It is important for us to understand how many records there are in each category of that variable. Histogram analysis gives us a visual representation of the distribution of records across different categories. This information is useful in understanding the important and most occurring categories in the data. It is also useful when splitting the training data for training, validation and testing as we need to ensure that all categories are sufficiently represented in all the splits.

Missing Values: Real-world data is much more challenging to analyze and process than sample data. In real cases, we may have several records with missing values for feature and label variables. These missing values for each variable need to be analyzed and appropriately handled. There are multiple options to handle the missing values and some of the considerations are highlighted below:

- Data is missing due to data collection issues: In the case of data fields that are missing due to incorrect/incomplete data collection procedure, missing information must be collected before starting further analysis.

- Default data/approximation: For the missing values, it might be possible to set the default values based on other fields in the record. However, the default option should not be overused if the particular value is missing for a large part of the dataset.

- Records with missing values can be omitted if these are a small percentage in the training data and do not represent any particular category. Deletion of records cannot be done, if missing values are large in number, as it will reduce the total data available for the model training.

- A particular feature variable can be removed if none of the above options work. Variables which only have few values do not add much predictive capability and hence can be removed from the model inputs. This option obviously cannot be used on the label variable.

Outliers: Outliers are the few data points that are outside the reasonable limits from the rest of the data. Outliers can happen either due to incorrect data capture, fraudulent data manipulation or genuine exceptional (or poor) performance. However, outliers can spoil the data analysis results and potentially reduce the accuracy of the machine learning models built on top of such data. Outliers can be identified from the distribution analysis described above. Let us say we are predicting the growth of the company based on previous 12 quarters' revenue growth:

Table 2. Sample Data for Outliers

Quarter	Company Growth (Q-o-Q)
Q1	4%
Q2	6%
Q3	3%
Q4	-7%
Q5	4%
Q6	6%
Q7	3%
Q8	4%
Q9	12%
Q10	6%
Q11	3%
Q12	4%

Simple visual inspection of the above data will tell us that there are 2 outliers. However, we cannot visually inspect large volume of data, so we need to work out the outliers based on the distribution analysis:

- Mean of the above data is 4.

- Variance of the above data is 16.66.

- Standard deviation of the above data is 4.08.

Considering that any data beyond one standard deviation is an outlier, it gives us 2 records which are outside the set zone. In our example, growth percentages above 8.08% (Mean + Standard deviation) and growth percentages below –0.08% are outliers. Q4 and Q9 are the only records which fall outside this range. Standard deviation computed without outlier records would have been just 1.18. Based on further analysis of these deviations, these outliers can be retained or removed from the training dataset. Datasets without the outliers give a much better basis for any further analysis and machine learning.

3.2 Multivariate Correlation Analysis

Multivariate correlation analysis is performed to understand the interdependencies between sets of variables in the training data. Correlation analysis is performed on the data from the following 2 dimensions:

– Correlation analysis between a feature variable and label variable is performed to understand the importance of that feature in explaining the label.

– Correlation analysis between sets of feature variables is performed to understand and minimize interdependencies between them.

Correlation analysis is dependent on the combination of types of variables to be analyzed.

Table 3. Multivariate Correlation Analysis

Type of variable 1	Type of variable 2	Analysis
Continuous	Continuous	Correlation Analysis
Categorical	Categorical	Distribution Analysis
Continuous	Categorical	Analysis of Variance

Let us look at each of these in detail.

Continuous vs. Continuous Variables: Correlation between 2 continuous variables is conceptually simple. We need to analyze and measure if the values in the 2 variables are moving together or in the opposite direction. Increase in the value of one variable resulting in an increase of the other variable indicates that they are positively correlated. In the opposite case of a decrease in the value of one variable on the increase of the other indicates that they are negatively correlated. Perfect correlations between training data variables are found only in academic examples but many possibilities can occur in real-life scenarios.

– Derivative of the feature is correlated to the label. For example, rate of change in profit may have a better correlation with market price and not the price itself.

- Feature has a correlation with the derivative of the label: Net profit has a correlation with change in the market price and not the price directly.

- Derivative of a feature has a correlation with the derivative of the label: Change in net profit has a correlation with change in the market price.

- Weighted average of a feature has a correlation with the label or derivative of the label: 200 day moving average of market price has a correlation with volatility.

- Temporal correlation: 3 consecutive quarters of profits growth trigger a significant change in the market price.

These scenarios indicate an innumerable number of combinations of data to be analyzed and complexity involved in selecting and engineering the features. Selection of machine learning algorithms can be relatively easy compared to the selection and presentation of the right features. In decision support use cases, this activity is intense as it requires a lot of domain knowledge and a trial and error approach.

Following are the techniques to quantify the correlation between 2 continuous variables in the training dataset. We use the following dataset for all the techniques so that we can understand the differences between the techniques. This dataset has 4 feature variables and 1 label. Through visual inspection, it can be seen that:

- Feature 1 and Label are perfectly correlated with linear relationship

- Feature 2 and Label are inversely correlated with linear relationship

- Feature 3 and Label are positively correlated with non-linear relationship

- Feature 4 and Label are inversely correlated with non-linear relationship

Table 4. Sample Continuous Data

Feature 1	Feature 2	Feature 3	Feature 4	Label
10	60	1	-1	1
20	50	4	-8	2
30	40	9	-27	3
40	30	16	-64	4
50	20	25	-125	5
60	10	36	-216	6

Let us see how each of the below methods fares on the above data.

Covariance: Covariance is a measure of correlation between the 2 variables. Positive covariance indicates that both the values move up together, and negative covariance indicates that these variables move in opposite directions. The absolute value of covariance has no significance compared to the sign of the value. Covariance computed on the above table results in:

- Covariance between Feature 1 and Label is 29.16 – indicating positive correlation

- Covariance between Feature 2 and Label is -29.16 – indicating negative correlation

- Covariance between Feature 3 and Label is 20.41 – indicating positive correlation

- Covariance between Feature 4 and Label is -121.91 – indicating negative correlation

This result is good as it indicates the direction of correlation but does not give a measure of it. We cannot estimate how highly correlated a pair of variables are from this metric.

Pearson Correlation: Pearson correlation is a normalized value of the covariance. Pearson correlation takes the value from -1 to 1. -1 indicates a perfect inverse linear correlation whereas

+1 reflects a perfect linear correlation. Zero value indicates no correlation. Like covariance, Pearson correlation does not capture non-linear relationships between variables. Let us look at the Pearson Correlation values.

- Pearson correlation between Feature 1 and Label is 1 – indicates perfect positive correlation

- Pearson correlation between Feature 2 and Label is –1 – indicates perfect negative correlation

- Pearson correlation between Feature 3 and Label is 0.97 – indicates positive correlation but is not able to capture the perfect non-linear correlation that exists between these variables

- Pearson correlation between Feature 4 and Label is 0.937 – indicates negative correlation but is not able to capture the inverse non-linear correlation that exists between these variables

Spearman Correlation: We have seen that Pearson correlation has limitations in capturing non-linear relationships between the variables. Spearman technique improvises on the Pearson coefficient to arrive at the non-linear relationships between the variables. It is a simple and effective concept. In this approach, all the values of the variables are ranked; the smallest value is ranked 1, the next is 2 and so on.

Pearson correlation in the previous section is computed on the ranks instead of actual values, giving us the Spearman correlation. This is basically to check if there is a linear correlation between the ranks of the values instead of the values themselves. High correlation on ranks indicates that these values go up or down together but maybe with different scales and hence can capture non-linear correlations. Table 5 contains the ranks of values within each variable from our example.

Table 5. Rank of the Features and Labels

Rank Feature 1	Rank Feature 2	Rank Feature 3	Rank Feature 4	Rank Label
1	6	1	6	1
2	5	2	5	2
3	4	3	4	3
4	3	4	3	4
5	2	5	2	5
6	1	6	1	6

- Spearman correlation between Feature 1 and Label is 1 – indicating positive correlation

- Spearman correlation between Feature 2 and Label is -1 – indicating inverse correlation

- Spearman correlation between Feature 3 and Label is 1 – indicating positive correlation

- Spearman correlation between Feature 4 and Label is -1 – indicating negative correlation

As you can see, Spearman correlation captures the non-linear relationships well. However, it cannot specify whether the relationship is linear or non-linear. So, it is important to compute and analyze a combination of the above methods to arrive at the conclusion.

Categorical vs. Categorical Variables: Categorical variable values can take one of the values from the list of categories. Two-way distribution analysis technique can be used to identify correlations between 2 categorical variables. Let us understand with an example data of student background, gender and their grades.

Table 6. Sample Student Data

Student	Background (Rural/Urban)	Gender (Male/Female)	Grade (A+, A, B, C)
Student 1	Rural	Male	A
Student 2	Urban	Female	A+
...	...	...	...
Student 180	Urban	Male	A

We have 2 feature variables—student background and gender—both are categorical. Student Grade, which is the label, is also a categorical value. Let us assume we have 180 student records and we need to analyze if there exists any correlation between:

- Gender vs. Grade

- Student background vs. Grade

This gives us an indication as to whether student background or gender have any predictive power in arriving at the grade.

Gender vs. Student Grade: As a first step in distribution analysis between 2 categorical variables, we need to summarize the data for each combination of values. For all possible values of gender and corresponding values of student grades, we need to arrive at the number of records. Table 7 contains the number of students for each combination of Gender and Student Grade variables.

Table 7. Student Data – Category-wise Summary

Gender	Student Grade	No of Students
M	A+	10
F	A+	10
M	A	20
F	A	20
M	B	38
F	B	42

Gender	Student Grade	No of Students
M	C	21
F	C	19
	Total	180

Then we need to compute the two-way distribution matrix for these variables. For each possible value of one variable, we compute the distribution of values in the other variable. In other words, for each grade, we compute the distribution of records across gender values and for each gender, we compute the distribution of records across grades.

In our example, A+ grades are distributed equally between male and female students with each of them getting 50% of those grades. We also need to compute the distribution analysis in the opposite direction. For every gender value, we need to compute the distribution of grades across students. Male student grades are distributed across A+, A, B and C, with a ratio of 11%, 22%, 43% and 24% respectively.

Two-way distribution analysis between Gender and Grade computed from the above-summarized data:

Table 8. Two-way Distribution Analysis

Grade\Gender	Male	Female	Total	Male	Female
	Grade-wise distribution across genders			Gender-wise distribution across grades	
A+	50%	50%	100%	11%	11%
A	50%	50%	100%	22%	22%
B	47%	53%	100%	43%	46
C	52%	48%	100%	24%	21%
			Total	100%	100%

Once we have the two-way distribution computed, correlations can be found out based on the distribution of records across categories. In the above table, each grade is more or less evenly distributed across genders (grade-wise distribution). Also, the distribution of grades across genders (gender-wise distribution) is also very similar. This indicates that the ratios of each category of the label are the same for each category of the feature. In other words, the value of gender has little or no impact on the grades. There is very little predictive power of the gender attribute in determining the expected grade.

Student Background vs. Grade: Let us look at the correlation between student background and Grade. Summarizing data for each student background and grade gives us the following table:

Table 9. Student Data – Category-wise Summary

Rural/Urban	Student Grade	No of Students
U	A+	15
R	A+	5
U	A	24
R	A	16
U	B	40
R	B	40
U	C	32
R	C	8
	Total	180

Two-way distribution analysis between student background and Grade is computed from the above table and captured here.

Table 10. Two-way Distribution Analysis

Grade\Background	Urban	Rural	Total	Urban	Rural
	Grade-wise distribution across backgrounds			Background-wise distribution of grades	
A+	75%	25%	100%	13%	8%
A	60%	40%	100%	26%	31%
B	50%	50%	100%	26%	46%
C	80%	20%	100%	35%	15%
			Total	100%	100%

From the above table, it can be seen that A+ and C grades are highly skewed toward urban students, whereas middle grades are evenly distributed (from grade-wise distribution analysis). Similarly, rural students have a much higher ratio of middle grades, i.e. 77% (31+46), compared to 52% (26+26) for urban students at the cost of fewer higher and bottom grades. From this table, we can infer that student background has definite predictive power on the grades.

Continuous vs. Categorical Variables: We can analyze the statistical summary of the continuous variable for each value of the categorical variable to arrive at the correlation between them. Earlier in the chapter, we looked at the statistical summary of continuous variables, which includes mean, median and standard deviation. Significant differences in the statistical summary across categories indicate a strong correlation between the variables and hence higher predictive capability. Statistical summary of the continuous variable similar across values of categorical variable indicates that there is no correlation between them.

Let us say we have an ice cream company that has 3 outlets in 3 different cities. Each outlet captures the daily sale value to be aggregated at the company level.

Table 11. Sample Sales Data

Outlet City	Day	Sales
City 1	Jan 1	100
City 2	Jan 1	90
......		
City 3	Dec 31	10

From the above table, we need to find out the correlations between:

- City and Sales

- Season and Sales

City and Sales: To arrive at the correlation, we need to compute the statistical summaries of the variable 'Sales' for the entire data as well as summaries for subsets of data for each city. Sample data is presented below.

Table 12. Distribution Analysis

Location	Highest Sale	Lowest Sale	Mean (Average)	Standard Deviation	Variance
Across Cities	200 units	10 units	60 units	40	1600
City 1	196 units	15 units	58 units	38	1444
City 2	200 units	12 units	62 units	41	1681
City 3	190 units	10 units	60 units	40	1600

From the above table, the distribution of sale information for each city is very similar to the distribution of overall information. Location is not giving us any predictive power as sales seem to be very similar across cities.

Season and Sales: Let us capture the statistical summaries of 'Sales' across seasons.

Table 13. Distribution Analysis

Season	Highest Sale	Lowest Sale	Mean (Average)	Standard Deviation	Variance
Across Seasons	200 units	10 units	60 units	40	1600
Season 1	200 units	120 units	160 units	20	400
Season 2	140 units	60 units	80 units	15	225
Season 3	60 units	10 units	30 units	20	400

We can see from this hypothetical example that the statistical summaries of sales are varying significantly across different seasons. Season has high predictive power in estimating the sales. At the company level, sale has a standard deviation of 40, which means that sale on any day deviates from the average sales by 40 units. We need to understand the features which contributed to such a deviation so that we can predict the sales on any day. Here we see the standard deviation across seasons is much smaller compared to the overall deviation. Season variable is able to explain a large part of the deviation in sales, whereas standard deviation across cities remained more or less the same. This is what is giving the predictive power to the season variable compared to the city variable.

3.3   Principal Component Analysis

Simple machine learning models perform better compared to complex ones. A model built on fewer feature variables is simpler compared to a model built on lots of them. Simpler models learn faster and can generalize better, thus improving the quality of predictions. As part of machine learning program, we may have access to a large number of feature variables and we need to zero in on few important variables so that the developed model is simple. This is also referred to as 'dimensionality reduction' as we are reducing the number of dimensions in the feature set.

One way to achieve dimensionality reduction is to perform correlation analysis, as described above, between each feature variable and the label to eliminate few non-important features. Alternatively, principal component analysis technique can be used to transform the contents of the feature variables into a new set of variables called principal components. There can be that many principal components as the number of original feature variables. However, principal components are ordered based on the relative importance of information held within each of them. Considering a subset of principal components consisting of top few of them for machine learning helps to reduce the dimension of the features without loss of information.

For a dataset with 'm' records, with each record having 'n' feature variables, principal component analysis produces a matrix of the same dimension, i.e. m records of n principal components. These 'n' principal components are presented in the descending order of influence. Let us take an example dataset of 6 records with 3 feature columns: age, dependents and salary, as shown in the table below.

Table 14. Sample Feature Data for PCA

Age	Dependents	Salary
24	0	1000
26	1	1200
30	1	1500
32	2	1800
38	2	2200
45	2	3000

Principal component analysis on the above data gives us the following result.

Table 15. Principal Component Values

Principal Component 1	Principal Component 2	Principal Component 3
-783.38032	0.191806	0.613211
-583.36954	0.270163	-0.21253
-283.344072	-0.513465	0.110211
16.660989	0.634166	-0.693914
416.702051	-1.075913	-0.22061
1216.730893	0.493243	0.403632

Principal components are not directly correlated to individual columns in the original dataset. Principal component 1 captures more information about the variance in the original data than component 2. Similarly, principal component 2 captures more information about the variance in the original data than component 3. So, we can build a machine learning algorithm to predict the Loan Eligibility based on just one feature variable—Principal Component 1—instead of 3 original features, achieving dimensionality reduction without losing much information.

How exactly does principal component analysis work? A data record with 'n' features can be visualized as a point in the 'n' dimensional space. For example, a customer record with 2 feature columns age and dependent information, say $(34, 2)$, can be plotted on a two-dimensional graph along x and y axes. Similarly, a data record with 3 features can be plotted on a three-dimensional graph along x, y, and z axes. In the principal component algorithm, existing data is projected to new axes instead of x, y, z axes. Here, we are not skipping or ignoring any data, but we are just presenting the data points using a different reference plane. Similar to our typical x-y-z plane, the new reference plane also has orthogonal axes, i.e. 90° angle to each other. We can visualize only three-dimensional plane, but the algorithm can be used for higher dimensional datasets as well.

The new axes are called eigenvectors and are computed in such a way that it extracts the inherent structure in the data. Data records projected onto the new axes are called principal components. The principal component algorithm computes 'n' principal components along 'n' eigenvectors from the data records of 'n' features. It is possible to re-compute the original data record from principal component analysis without any loss of information. The algorithm also provides the relative importance of the data in each eigenvector by computing 'eigenvalues' for each principal component.

The principal component with the highest eigenvalue provides the maximum explanation for the variance in the data, followed by the second principal component and then the third and so on. This gives us the option to consider only the first few important principal components into our model, ignoring remaining values without much loss of information. As we have seen earlier, the process of reducing the number of features by ignoring less important ones is referred to as dimensionality reduction.

Visual Example: Let us look at figure 8 in which two-dimensional feature data is represented in a typical graph with x and y axes.

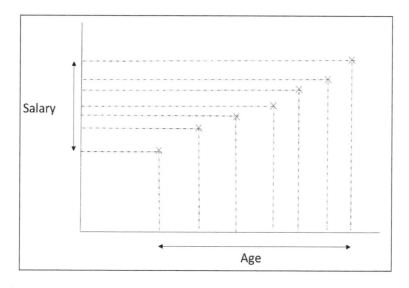

Figure 8. Two-dimensional Data Presented as a Graph

In this figure, both the dimensions are important for preserving the information as the projection of data points on either axis is widely spread. We will lose a lot of information if we were to ignore either of the features in order to achieve dimensionality reduction. Figure 9 gives a view of the remaining data if we were to ignore one dimension.

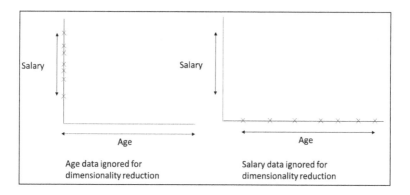

Figure 9. Single Dimension View of the Two-Dimensional Data

We lose more information when we ignore age (x-axis), as the variance of data along the x-axis is higher compared to the y-axis. However, the y-axis too has considerable information to ignore.

Principal component analysis identifies a new plane in such a way that a line that explains the maximum variance for the given data forms the new x-axis. This is followed by identifying a plane perpendicular to the new axis which can explain the next best variance in the data. This exercise is done for all the dimensions in the data in the descending order of importance. Principal component analysis gives us these new dimensions which are orthogonal (at 90 degrees angle) to each other. These new axes are also called eigenvectors. PCA also gives us the order of importance of these eigenvectors in explaining the variance in the given data. This sorting order is based on the 'eigenvalues' computed by the algorithm.

Eigenvectors are new axes in place of x-y-z and when the data is projected onto this new plane, it has the potential to explain the variance better. Eigenvalues indicate the importance of each eigenvector in explaining the variance in the data. Data projected onto eigenvector is called principal components. Principal components are numbered based on the descending order of eigenvalues. Data projected to eigenvector with the highest eigenvalue is called principal component 1 and the lowest eigenvalue is called principle component n (n being the number of dimensions in the data).

For the above example, we can see in figure 10 that PCA algorithm computes the eigenvectors and the original data is projected onto the new plane.

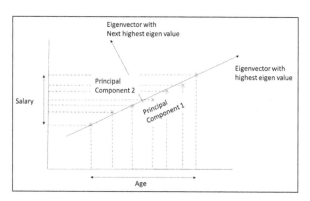

Figure 10. Principal Component Axes

Figure 11 depicts the view of the original data mapped to new planes derived by PCA algorithm. Our original age vs. salary data has been mapped to principal component 1 vs. principal component 2. As we can see from the figure, principal component 1 explains the maximum variance in the data and hence holds the maximum information. Principal component 2 has little variance and can be ignored without much loss of information. We have simply mapped the coordinates of the original points to new planes and in that process, we have not lost any information. We can derive the original data points by simply mapping the new data points to the original axes.

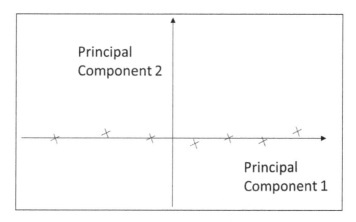

Figure 11. Original Data Projected Along Principal Component Axes

Let us project the data by ignoring less the important feature, 'principal component 2.' We can see from figure 12 that this will not result in any loss of information.

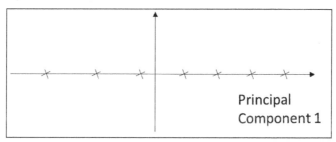

Figure 12. Single Dimension View of the Data Along Principal Component 1

Once we have mapped the data to principal components, we can retain the first few principal components and ignore the remaining ones. Let us say we have a 5-feature data mapped to 5-dimensional principal components, we can retain first 2 or 3 dimensions and ignore the remaining. Thus, we have effectively reduced a 5-feature dataset into a 2 or 3 feature dataset.

PCA algorithm works perfectly well for much higher dimensional data as well and it significantly helps to reduce the dimensions of the feature vector. Reduced dimensions for the feature vector mean simple models for machine learning which can generalize the prediction.

3.4   Data Pre-Processing

Machine learning algorithms always take numerical data as the features and label. Machine learning algorithms cannot process strings, images, date or any other data structure in its original form. It is necessary to convert all the inputs into some form of numerical values as part of pre-processing for efficient learning.

Continuous Variables: These are the variables that take any value of input within a given range like age, price and marks. These variables are either in integer or float formats. We need to normalize or bin them as part of pre-processing.

> **Normalization:** Some machine learning algorithms expect input to be in a given a range for the learning to happen. Also, the range of values in different feature variables needs to be on a comparable scale. Age with range 0–100 and salary with range 0–100,000 may skew the results. Normalization is done to ensure that the above problems are addressed. Normalization techniques are discussed in the next subsection.

> **Binning:** Sometimes, processing the numerical data as is may not be required. The merchant may prefer to know the purchase patterns for an age group rather than every age. Binning is a

technique to convert the continuous value into a categorical value. For example, age value can be converted into 3 buckets: Teen. Middle-aged and Senior. Binning can be done using several methods like:

- User-specified ranges – (Teen is 13–19, Senior is 60 +, etc.)

- Equal range bins – (A category of every 5-year range 0–5 years, 5–10 years)

- Equal size bins – (Top 25% of the students are top performers, bottom 25% are poor performers, etc.)

Categorical Variables: These are the variables that can take one of the possible values from the list of categories. As part of pre-processing, we need to encode the categorical values so that machine learning algorithms can process the data better. We may also need to group the categories further to reduce the overall number of categories for the feature.

Grouping of Categories: For some categorical values, the number of possible values may be too large to make any meaningful contribution to the learning. For example, products in a store or postcode. There are too many products in a store or postcodes to make any meaningful inference in the learning phase. These values can be grouped to get fewer categories depending on the objective of the learning. Postcodes may be grouped across regions and products may be grouped based on category or price range.

Encoding: Categorical values contain a numerical or string representation of the category they belong to. Student grade can be 'A+,' 'A,' 'B' or 'C.' These features need to be encoded for efficient learning. A common method used for encoding categorical values is called one-hot encoding, in which one binary variable is given for each possible category values.

For example, customer ordering location variable can take 1 of the 5 possible values: 'metro,' 'city,' 'district,' 'town' and 'village.'

Each of the possible values is represented by a binary indicator. A feature value is represented by a vector of binary values. Encoded values for customer ordering location are presented in the below table.

Table 16. One-Hot Encoding

Category	Value 1	Value 2	Value 3	Value 4	Value 5
Metro	1	0	0	0	0
City	0	1	0	0	0
District	0	0	1	0	0
Town	0	0	0	1	0
Village	0	0	0	0	1

Each feature is represented by 5 digits; City is represented by 01000 whereas village is represented by 00001. As each value has one positive value and remaining as zeroes, these are called sparse vectors or sparse representation.

3.5 Normalization Techniques

Normalization of numerical data is required mainly for the following reasons:

- Some machine learning models function effectively when the inputs are in a given range of values, for example values in the range of –3 and +3. For the input values beyond the specified range, the output of some non-linear functions in neural networks is not responsive to the changes in the input.

- Scaling the different numerical elements to a common range so that no particular variable can unduly influence the model. For example, table 17 captures the sample data used for analyzing the impact of age and income on the monthly expenses.

Table 17. Sample Data for Normalization

Age	Income	Expense
24	100,000	40,000
42	120,000	75,000
62	80,000	60,000

Values for income are 1000x bigger than the values of age. In some machine learning models, variables with higher values may have a higher impact in the training, neutralizing the impact of smaller attributes on the expected outcome. Need and approach for normalization are dependent on the chosen machine learning model and the training approach.

Here are the most common normalization techniques used:

Min-Max Normalization: Min-max normalization of a feature converts continuous data of feature values into a range 0 to 1. The smallest value in the feature data is mapped to zero and the largest value is mapped to 1. All the remaining are allocated a value on a pro-rata basis between 0 and 1. Such transformed data captures the relative size of the feature across different records, omitting the absolute values. Min-Max normalization when applied to multiple variables, eliminates the size disparity while leaving the relative sizes of the values. Table 18 gives an example of min-max normalized values for a given feature.

Table 18. Min-Max Normalization

Feature Value	Min-Max Normalized Value
40	0.016
21	0
25	0.003
60	0.033
34	0.011
1200	1
250	0.194
475	0.385

Sigmoid Normalization: This method normalizes the feature data of any value to a range between 0 and 1. This normalization uses the sigmoid function, which has an effective range of feature values approximately between -3 and 3. Feature values below -3 are normalized to a value very close to zero. Similarly, feature values above 3 are normalized to a value very close to 1. Sigmoid normalization is not really effective when the feature data is not within the range specified above. Let us look at an example of sigmoid normalization.

Table 19. Sigmoid Normalization

Feature Value	Sigmoid Normalized Value
-30	9.35762E-14
-10	4.53979E-05
-3	0.047425873
2	0.880797078
1	0.731058579
0	0.5
1	0.731058579
2	0.880797078
3	0.952574127
10	0.999954602
30	1

Log Normalization: In this method, original feature data is transformed using the logarithm function. Log normalization scales down the feature exponentially and makes the data values comparable. Log normalization cannot be applied on features with negative values. Let us look at an example.

Table 20. Log Normalization

Feature Value	Log Normalized Value
0.000001	-6
0.0001	-4
0.01	-2
0.1	-1

Feature Value	Log Normalized Value
100	2
1000	3
100000	5
10000000	7

In the above example, feature values have a very wide range, with the highest value billions of times higher than the lowest value. Such a large range of values can cause issues in training the machine learning model. On the other hand, log normalized values of the feature have a linear increase.

Normalization techniques ensure that the quantum of values of the features do not adversely impact the learning and help in faster training and superior results.

4

Pre-Processing of Unstructured Data

In the last chapter, we looked at the analyzing and pre-processing of structured data. Structured data is predominantly used in decision support use cases of machine learning. For cognitive use cases like machine vision, speech and natural language processing, the data is in an unstructured form. Machine learning algorithms can only process numerical data in a structured form and cannot process text messages or videos directly. Hence, unstructured data in the form of text, sound, images and video needs to be pre-processed. As part of pre-processing, we need to convert unstructured data into a structured format that can be used for training.

Unlike structured data, we do not need to analyze correlations in cognitive use cases as there is a definite natural correlation between an image or text and what can be inferred from them. For example, we need to analyze how much impact weather has on ice cream sales, but we can be sure that contents of the image are sufficient to decide whether the picture contains a human face or not. Pre-processing of images, videos and sounds is relatively simpler compared to processing of unstructured text. Natural language text can be correctly understood only in the right context and comes with complexities related to languages, grammar and synonyms. In this chapter, we will look at the pre-processing required for unstructured data like text and multimedia.

4.1 Text Processing

Unstructured text in the form of reports, websites, tweets and reviews needs to be pre-processed in a way that machine language algorithms can understand and analyze. Some of the use cases for text processing are:

- Understanding the sentiment of a message/tweet/review

- Natural Language Search

- Natural Language Translation

- Information Extraction

Machine learning model for natural text processing requires the following steps:

- Extraction and Tokenization: Words and sentences from the text need to be extracted from the document or report or tweet.

- Word Representation: Text needs to be presented in numerical form to the machine learning model using a mapping representation.

- Machine Learning Model: Regression or classification algorithm need to be structured for the given problem.

Extraction and Tokenization: Natural language processing requires various parts of the text like words and sentences to be extracted and tagged. 'Natural Language Toolkit' (NLTK) is a popular open source platform with a suite of text processing libraries. Following are some of the functions for text processing.

> **Word Tokenization**: Word tokenization extracts each word from the document into a data structure. Word tokenization considers aspects like punctuation marks, salutations, names and special characters to arrive at a word-wise breakup of the text.

Sentence Tokenization: Sentence tokenization is the process of splitting the document into separate sentences. Sentence tokenization is useful in use cases like natural language translation.

Parts of Speech (POS): This component tags each and every word extracted from the document with a POS label like noun, verb or adjective. Parts of speech tagging can be used in preparing the data for use cases. For example, a sentiment analysis model can be built on the 'adjective' words alone from the text, ignoring all other POS words.

Stop Words: Stop words are commonly used word like 'a,' 'an,' 'the,' etc. which can be ignored for many of the use cases. Stop words can be removed from the text without losing the meaning.

Lemmatizing: Lemmatizing is about removing additional characters added to a word depending on the usage. For example, 'travelling,' 'travels,' 'travelled' are all replaced by 'travel' as part of lemmatizing. Lemmatizing helps to ensure that different usages of the same word are processed and understood in the same manner.

Named Entity Recognition: Natural language text contains names of people, organizations, places and miscellaneous other things. Extracted words from the text are tagged with the type of entity if the word belongs to one of the named entities. This information is used in training the model.

Word Representation: Words or sentences cannot be presented as is to the machine learning model and need to be converted into numerical values. There are several techniques to represent words or sentences in numerical form so that the machine learning algorithm can learn and interpret. Following are some such techniques:

Model Dictionary: Building a dictionary for the machine learning model is the process of extracting all the unique words from all the given training documents, tweets or reviews. A dictionary may be created with all the words from the training dataset or a subset of words based on tags associated with the words. Some possible options are:

- All words from all the training documents.

- All words from all the training documents except stop words like 'a,' 'an,' 'the.'

- All words tagged as 'adjectives' or 'adverb' in POS tagging.

All the unique words from all the documents along with the count of their appearance are stored as part of the dictionary. Count of the appearance of unique words can be used in 2 ways:

- Model dictionary may be subset based on the occurrence frequency of the words. For example, a model dictionary created for a set of research reports may have 25000 words, but we may subset that to 1000 most frequently occurring words to make the size of the dictionary manageable.

- Count of appearance of words can be used to normalize the relevance of occurrence of a word. For example, a single occurrence of a rare word may have higher weightage than a single occurrence of a frequently occurring word.

One-Hot Encoding: One-hot encoding is a sparse representation of words in a dictionary. Each word is represented by a vector of size 'n' where n is the number of words in the model dictionary. For example, a model dictionary with 10 words needs a vector of 10 binary values, with each value catering to a word in the dictionary. A word is represented by marking the corresponding value in the vector as '1,' leaving the remaining value as zero. Table 21 depicts the one-hot encoding representation for a dictionary of 10 words.

Table 21. One-Hot Encoding Representation of Words

Word	One-hot Encoding
Word 1	1000000000
Word 2	0100000000
Word 3	0010000000
Word 4	0001000000
Word 5	0000100000
Word 6	0000010000
Word 7	0000001000
Word 8	0000000100
Word 9	0000000010
Word 10	0000000001

As each representation has only a single '1' with all remaining zeroes, it is called sparse representation. As each word is represented by that many number of digits as the number of words in the dictionary, one-hot encoding is not the efficient way for representation of text.

Bag-of-Words: We have seen that capturing large documents using one-hot encoding can be very inefficient as each word can be a very large sparse representation. However, certain use cases like sentiment analysis or e-mail filtering do not require an exact sequence of words. It is enough to find whether a certain word occurred or not and if so, how many times. Bag-of-words representation for a given document captures the number of times each word in the model dictionary appeared in the document. Table 22 captures a sample bag-of-words representation.

Table 22. Bag-of-Words Representation

Document	Number of occurrences of words in the dictionary							
	Word1	Word2	Word3	Word4	Word5	...	...	Word10
Document 1	2	1	1	1	2	0	0	...
Document 2	4	1	5	2	1	3	0	4

In one-hot encoding, each word is represented by a sparse vector of the size of the model dictionary. However, in bag-of-words, each document is represented by a vector of the same size. This approach does not capture the sequence of words but just the count or occurrence of the same.

Word2Vec: We have seen that one-hot encoding makes the representation size very large whereas bag-of-words representation addresses that problem but misses out information on the relative position of words. Word2vec is a way of representing each word in the form of a dense vector. In one-hot encoding representation, the size of each word is determined by the number of words in the dictionary. However, in word2vec, vector size is designed to be much smaller. For example, a dense 4-digit vector can represent up to 10,000 words, which would need 10,000 binary variables to represent in one-hot encoding.

Neural networks can be used to automatically extract the features from unstructured data like text and images. Word2vec representation is built using a 2-layer neural network from the given training documents and model dictionary. Word2vec representation also captures the semantic meaning of the terms apart from unique representation. We can run mathematical formulas on vector representation of words just like we run formulas on numbers. A popular example for mathematical formula on word2vec representation of words is:

King – Male + Female = Queen.

Vector representation of the word 'Male,' when subtracted from the vector for 'King' and added with the vector for 'Female,' ends up in a point very close to the vector representation of 'Queen.' Word2vec not only helps to represent words in a dense vector but also helps in capturing the semantic meanings better.

4.1 Multimedia Processing

Multimedia files like images and videos have raw data in the form of pixel density which can be processed by machine learning algorithms.

Images: The MNIST database is a large collection of handwritten digits commonly used for benchmarking image processing machine learning models. MNIST's handwritten digit recognition problem is the "Hello World" equivalent in machine learning parlance. MNIST database consists of handwritten digits of size 28 × 28 pixels, which can be represented as arrays of 784 pixels (28 × 28) for training.

However, for image recognition problems, it is best to represent the images as two-dimensional data so that spatial relationships between different pixels can be preserved as part of training. Deep learning algorithms like convolutional neural networks expect the data to be in the original two-dimensions space. This is in line with how we humans perceive the images as two-dimensional information and not as a series of pixels.

Source images may be in different formats like gray scale, RGB or CMYK. Data representation for each pixel changes depending on the image format. For non-gray scale images, each pixel may have multiple values. In the case of RGB images, each pixel has 3 values indicating the weights of Red, Green and Blue colors in that pixel. The source image can be converted to gray scale image before taking the pixel density for processing if color values are not important for the use case.

Video Processing: Video files are nothing but images captured at a certain rate of frames per second so that it gives the visual perception of movement. Open source tools like FFmpeg provide a number of features to manipulate video files including

- Separate the video and audio contents
- Split the video into a series of image frames

Images and sounds can be processed separately as per the techniques described above.

Typical use cases for video processing involve:

- Video surveillance: Identification of people from video signals and compare with the specimen images.

- Machine Vision: Identification of objects and movements from a streaming video.

- Video Tagging: Tagging the videos into one of the specified categories.

Open Source Computer Vision Library (OpenCV) is an open source computer vision and machine learning library built to provide common infrastructure for computer vision applications. The library has over 2500 algorithms to detect and recognize faces, identify objects, track moving objects and so on.

5

Parametric Regression Techniques

Regression techniques predict the output of a continuous numerical value based on the training performed using historical training data. Predicting the product sales, student marks, stock index or rainfall are examples of regression use cases. There are several machine learning techniques to perform regression. In this chapter, we will look at parametric regression techniques.

Parametric regression techniques function based on the assumption that the output value can be derived from the values of the input data. Each input feature contributes some part of the output value, which, when combined together for all features, gives the output. Some input feature values contribute more to the output value than others. Impact of each input feature value on output is captured in the form of 'weight' or 'parameter' for that feature.

As part of training a parametric regression model, the relationship between pairs of inputs and corresponding outputs in the historical data is estimated. Training techniques help in computing the weights of different inputs to arrive at the computed result which is as close the historical output as possible. These weights form the regression model using which future predictions can be made.

5.1   Linear Regression Example

Regression is about building a mathematical model based on the historical data and using the same to project the future outcomes. Linear regression methods assume that output is linearly proportional to each input but weightage of contribution of each input may vary. Let us look at a simple linear regression example.

We have the following information about historical ice cream sales and maximum temperature of the day from an ice cream parlor.

Table 23. Sample Data for Linear Regression

Maximum Temperature	Actual Ice Cream Sales
0	4
5	5
10	6
20	44
25	46
30	64
35	74

Firstly, we can do a quick check to ensure that the data is suitable for linear regression. Visual inspection of the data shows that there is a strong correlation between the variables. We can also validate the same by computing Pearson correlation for the data. The easiest way to compute Pearson correlation is using the 'PEARSON' formula in Excel. Pearson correlation between temperature and ice cream sales is 0.975, indicating a strong linear correlation between the 2 variables.

Linear regression is performed using the 'ordinary least squares' method. We will look at the algorithm in detail in the next section. Linear regression using 'ordinary least squares' can be performed using the Excel formula 'LINEST.' In a training dataset with 'n' features and 1 label, LINEST produces a constant and 'n' weights. Linear regression on the above data with 1 feature and 1 label gives us the following output:

Computed Constant = −4.42666

Weight for Temperature = 2.191781

From this regression output, prediction formula for ice cream sales can be defined as:

Ice Cream Sales = −4.42666 + 2.191781 * Temperature

Using this formula, we can predict ice cream sales for any given temperature.

Figure 13 depicts the actual ice cream sales and estimated sales by the regression algorithm. This algorithm can be used further to estimate the ice cream sales for any day given the temperature on that day.

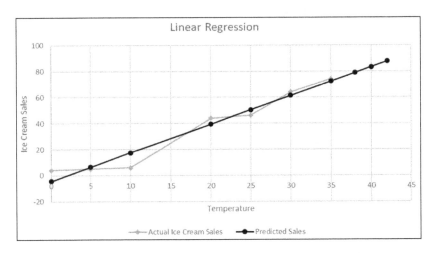

It is interesting to note that the computed line does not match with any of the actual points, but ordinary least squares algorithm ensures that the combined error of the regression formula across training records is minimum. Prediction using parametric regression techniques is a mathematical formula of the corresponding input values and it does not depend on the historical outputs directly.

Ice Cream Sales = Bias + Weight * Temperature

In the above example, the formula just contains the inputs for the current record but does not include historical sales.

Some regression algorithms like k-nearest neighbor and random forest consider historical output into the computation of prediction. These models have the inherent capability to capture non-linear relationships and do not have weighted parameters for each input.

5.2   Ordinary Least Squares (OLS)

Linear regression is a parametric model in which we assign a weighted parameter for each of the inputs. We will see later in the book neural networks and deep learning algorithms which are much more complex but again are parametric in nature. Machine learning algorithms rely on linear algebra and differentiation techniques to train these parametric models.

Fundamental Concepts: Some fundamental concepts before getting into the algorithm.

Let us say we have a variable Y which is dependent on variable X.

$$Y = f(X)$$

This dependency can be a linear, quadratic or complex-nonlinear dependency.

Linear dependency is represented by the following equation:

$$Y = mX + c, \text{ where m and C are constants.}$$

For linear regression, we are assuming such a linear relationship between output and inputs.

Quadratic dependency is represented by the following equation:

$$Y = aX^2 + bX + c$$

Complex non-linear relationships can take any form with a combination of polynomial, logarithmic or trigonometric function.

Figure 14 captures the visualization of linear, quadratic and complex non-linear relationships between Y and X.

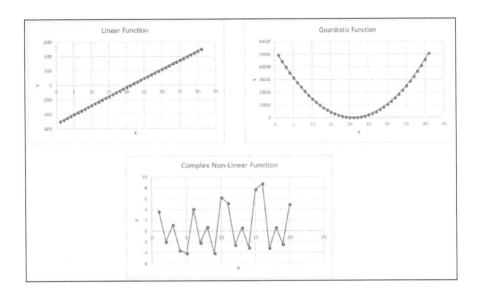

Figure 14. Visualization of Linear, Quadratic and Complex Non-Linear Functions

As we can see from the above diagram, quadratic functions are always convex with a global minimum. In other words, there is always a single value of the independent variable at which the dependent variable is at its minimum. It is not the case with complex non-linear functions which are not convex and can have several minima.

The derivative of output Y with respect to X indicates the amount of change in Y when there is a small change in the value of X. For quadratic equations, the derivative tends to be zero at global minimum, as they are convex in nature. So, the minimum can be found by simply computing the derivatives and equating it to zero. For non-linear complex functions, as there is no single global minimum, we have to run an incremental optimization algorithm like 'gradient descent' to arrive at the possible minima.

OLS Algorithm: Ordinary least squares algorithm expresses the error in the training data as a quadratic cost function of weights. As explained in the fundamentals above, quadratic functions have a global minimum which can be computed by equating the derivative of the function to zero. OLS algorithm finds the optimum weights by computing the derivatives of the quadratic cost function for each weight and equating the same to zero. Let us look at it in a bit more detail.

In the linear regression model, the output can be represented as:

Prediction output = Function (weights, historical inputs)

Here, we need to compute ideal weights in such a way that error between the historical output and prediction output is minimized.

Ordinary least squares technique defines the cost as a quadratic function:

$$\text{Cost} = (\text{historical output} - \text{prediction output})^2$$

Rewriting by combining the above 2 formulas:

$$\text{Cost} = (\text{historical output} - \text{weights} * \text{historical inputs})^2$$

For the given dataset, historical input and output values are given. So, the above equation can be viewed as:

$$\text{Cost} = (\text{Constant1} + \text{Weights} * \text{Constant 2})^2$$

This is a quadratic equation which has a global minimum for cost, which can be found out by computing cost derivative over each weight and equating the same to zero. Ordinary least squares model predicts the output for all the given inputs in such a way that mean squared error is minimized.

Following are the implication of using OLS cost for regression:

- Positive and negative errors are considered the same as we are using the square function. Cost will be the same irrespective of whether predicted sales is 10% above or below the actual sales.

- Large errors are given higher weightage than small errors. 4 units of difference between prediction and actual output is 16 times more cost than 1 unit of difference. Due to this, outliers in the data can have much higher influence and adversely impact the regression line.

Similar to linear regression, there are also non-linear regression techniques which are parametric in nature. These models are built using similar differentiation techniques discussed for linear regression.

Polynomial Regression: Polynomial regression computes the weights for each feature as well as weights for polynomials of the features. It can be specified to include up to the nth polynomial for each feature. Here, we are basically adding additional derived features consisting of polynomials of original features. This can capture non-linear relationships between the features and label more effectively. However, OLS algorithm works exactly like linear regression, with the difference being that polynomial regression has more features and hence more weights to compute.

Exponential/Logarithmic Regression: In this regression, constant and weights are computed in such a way that the result is the multiple of constant and weights raised to the value of each variable.

Ordinary least squares is a simple and useful tool but has certain disadvantages and does not result in the best solution in the following scenarios:

- Outliers in the training data

- Correlations between the input variables

- Large number of input variables with few training data records

- Non-linear and complex relationships between inputs and outputs other than polynomial or logarithmic

5.3   Regularization Techniques

Parametric models have certain inherent limitations. As part of training the model, we are training weights for each and every feature. Data records with a large number of features end up with a large number of parameters. We use linear algebra and differentiation techniques to find out optimum weights to minimize the cost function. A large number of features with a limited number of training records results in a suboptimal model. Correlations between the feature variables result in synchronized changes in the corresponding weight parameters, which is not desirable. A large number of weights means a complex model. It is always preferable to have a simple model if it gives comparable results with that of a complex model, as simple models generalize better.

Regularization is a process of controlling the parameters as part of training. Remember the ordinary least squares cost function discussed earlier.

OLS Cost = (historical output – weights * historical inputs) ^{2}

We have only one constraint to optimize the weights, i.e. minimizing the cost function. Regularization is about placing an additional constraint on the cost function.

Regularized OLS Cost = (historical output – weights * historical inputs) ^{2} + function (All weights)

With the above equation, we are not just interested in finding the weights for minimizing the cost but also minimize the values of the weights overall. As we train the model to optimize the above cost function, it modifies the weights in such a way that it is not only bringing the error down but also the values of the weights. With this approach, only the weights of most important feature variables are retained while other weights are reduced to a minimum.

There are broadly 2 regularized regression algorithms.

Lasso Regression: In this regression, the simple addition of all weights is added to the OLS cost.

Regularized OLS Cost = (historical output – weights * historical inputs) ^{2} + Sum (weights)

Ridge Regression: In this regression, squares of all weights are aggregated and added to the OLS cost.

$$\text{Regularized OLS Cost} = (\text{historical output} - \text{weights} * \text{historical inputs})^2 + \text{Sum (weights}^2)$$

It is important to note that cost function in both lasso and ridge regression is quadratic in nature and can be solved by equating the derivative of cost function for each weight to zero. Regularization is a very useful technique not only in regression but even in other parametric learning techniques like neural networks and deep learning. We will discuss this further in the next chapters.

5.4   Logistic Regression

Logistic regression works on the same mathematical principles as that of ordinary least square linear regression. However, logistic regression is used to arrive at an output of type binary. For example, logistic regression can be used to predict whether a student will pass or fail the exam based on the number of hours of study. Historical output for logistic regression can take binary values of 0 or 1 instead of a continuous value. Similarly, the prediction from logistic regression has to be binary in nature. To achieve this, an exponential function called logit function is used to convert the weighted inputs to binary form.

Logit function can take any numerical value as input and produce an output value between 0 and 1. Binary prediction is arrived at based on the output of the logit function.

$$\text{Prediction output} = 0 \text{ if Logit (inputs, parameters)} < 0.5$$
$$= 1 \text{ if Logit (inputs, parameters)} > 0.5$$

Cost function for logistic regression can be least squares cost function.

$$\text{Cost} = (\text{Historical actual output} - \text{Logit (weights} * \text{inputs}))^2$$

As part of the training, the algorithm selects the optimum parameters so that cost is reduced, and hence maximum records are correctly classified into one of the binary outputs. It is important to note that cost function here is not a quadratic function and hence does not have a global minimum. So, optimization algorithms like gradient descent need to be used to arrive at the optimal weights to minimize the cost. The logit function is also called as sigmoid and it acts as an activation function in neural networks. We will discuss sigmoid function and gradient descent optimization technique in the chapter *Neural Networks*.

6

Decision Trees and Forests

6.1   Introduction

Flowcharts are a popular tool for capturing decision rules. Flowcharts are created by business subject matter experts (SMEs) and are represented as a series of decision criteria leading to the recommended action. Decision trees are similar to flowcharts but are automatically developed by the machine learning algorithm from the historical training data. Decision trees are a series of condition checks arranged in a hierarchical manner such that when these checks are performed on the data record, it leads to the prediction.

Figure 15 represents a sample decision tree to arrive at the probability of loan repayment.

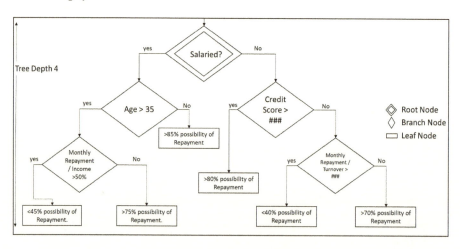

Figure 15. Sample Decision Tree

76

Key points about decision trees:

- Decision trees start with root node at the top and leaf node at the bottom.

- Root node is the starting node for evaluation of the record.

- Decision trees may have several branch nodes in between root node and leaf node.

- All nodes, except leaf nodes, represent a check to be performed on the given data.

- Leaf nodes are at the bottom of the tree and contain prediction.

- Decision trees are binary in nature, i.e. all nodes branch into exactly 2 child nodes except leaf nodes.

- Decision trees are intuitive, and it is relatively easy to get to the decision.

- Decision trees have the capability to explain the rationale behind the prediction.

Let us look at the important terms of the decision tree.

Root Node: This is the top of the tree and contains the most important condition for the given training data.

Branch Node: Each condition is represented as a branch node. Training algorithm chooses the best condition to split the data based on the training data.

Leaf Node: Leaf is at the bottom of the tree and contains the prediction.

Height: Height of the tree is the maximum number of branches between the root node and leaf node. Decision trees are not symmetrical. Some predictions are done after fewer decisions than others. The maximum height of a tree is a hyperparameter for training the decision trees.

Maximum no. of Nodes: Indicates the total number of nodes in a decision tree. This is also a hyperparameter.

Minimum no. of Items in a Leaf: Decision trees cannot have a series of decisions for each record. Such a model is memorizing the data and not generalizing. Minimum number of items in a leaf node ensures that the model does not overfit the training data. Minimum number of items in a leaf node is a hyperparameter.

6.2   Information Theory

Decision tree algorithm uses the concept of 'entropy' from information theory to build the trees. In real life, we make decisions based on the information available to us. We are more confident when we have sufficient information for making the decision but feel jittery when we have no information to decide. Can we quantify the amount of information we have?

Amount of information we have about a particular event can be measured by the mathematical term 'entropy.' Entropy indicates a lack of information about an event, which is the inverse of the amount of information we know. High entropy means we have very little information to take a decision and low entropy means we can be confident about our decisions.

Entropy can take a value from 0 to 1 for use cases with binary outcomes. For use cases with n possible outcomes entropy can take a value from 0 to $\text{Log}_2 n$

Table 24. Entropy Values

Entropy Value	What It Means
0	We are 100% sure about the outcome
0.5	50% chance of positive result
1	We know nothing about the outcome

Entropy is arrived at based on the probabilities computed from historical training data. Let us see the value of entropy in predicting the outcome of a flipped coin. We have no information about the outcome of a flipped coin assuming it is a fair coin. So, it is 50% chance of heads and 50% chance of tails. For this prediction, computed entropy is 1, which correctly indicates that we have no information about the outcome.

Let us take another example. We are expected to predict whether a plane arrives on time or not. Consider the following scenarios:

- Scenario 1: We do not have any information (50% chance of coming on time)

- Scenario 2: We know that across the globe, airlines on-time performance is 80% (80% chance of coming on time)

- Scenario 3: We know that our specific airline on-time performance is 90% (90% chance of coming on time)

- Scenario 4: We know that our airline on-time performance in this airport is 95% (95% chance of coming on time)

Let us look at computed entropy in these 4 scenarios.

Table 25. Entropy – Sample Scenarios

Scenario	Description	Entropy
1	No information	1
2	Globally airline on-time performance	0.72
3	Our airline on-time performance	0.46
4	Our airline on-time performance in this report	0.28

It is evident from this hypothetical example that as we gather more information, we are reducing the entropy of our prediction. Loss of entropy shows we have additional information, which is also called information gain. Entropy and information gain are used in the decision tree algorithm to arrive at the decision hierarchy. Those conditions that give maximum information gain are placed at the top of the tree.

6.3 Decision Tree Algorithm

Decision tree algorithm also has the following steps:

- Model building – building decision tree

- Prediction from the model

Model Building: Decision tree algorithm is a supervised machine learning technique. This algorithm builds the decision tree from the given training dataset consisting of multiple features and corresponding label. Model building in decision tree algorithm involves arriving at hierarchical conditions from the given training data in such a way that these conditions lead to the leaf node with correct prediction.

Unlike a real tree, a decision tree has its root at the top and grows downwards. The most important check in predicting the label is performed at the top of the tree/root node. Based on this check, data is split into 2 branches and the algorithm computes the next most important condition for splitting the data for both branches separately. The height of the tree represents the number of layers of nodes in the tree. In figure 15, given above, we have 4 levels of nodes; hence the height of the tree is 4. Decision tree algorithm stops creating more nodes whenever it reaches the following conditions:

- No more splits of the data possible. All the records ending up at a leaf node belonging to the same category.

- Limit on maximum depth/height of the tree is reached.

- Minimum records per node is reached, even though all records are not homogeneous.

- Limit on maximum number of nodes is reached.

A tree is grown using the above logic until all the training records are placed in a leaf node or one of the limits mentioned above is reached.

A tree built without any limits on depth, records per node or number of nodes is called a fully grown tree. Fully grown trees have zero training error when predicting the outcome for the training dataset. This is an indication of overfitting and hence such trees do not generalize the prediction. Above limits specified on the tree building algorithm ensures generalization and superior prediction even though such limits introduce error when predicting the outcome for the training dataset.

Training error is a result of the fact that training data records at each leaf node are not completely homogeneous for the decision trees that are not fully grown. For leaf nodes with records that are not homogenous, the prediction is based on the average output across the different records in that node. Prediction for classification of a new record in such cases is taken as the middle value ('Mode') of the labels of the records in that leaf node. For a regression problem, the average of all the labels of the records of the given leaf node is taken as the prediction.

Pruning of trees is a technique to reduce the complexity of the trees by reducing the number of nodes in the tree without impacting the total training error. There are several techniques to achieve pruning. Pruning process starts at each leaf node and combines both branches if it does not impact the overall error of the tree. Pruning ensures less complex trees and hence generalization.

Prediction Using the Model: Once the tree is built, generating predictions from the tree is a relatively simple process of evaluating the given input record for each condition starting at the root node and navigating through the hierarchy until the leaf node is reached.

Each leaf node represents a prediction. For classification problems, leaf node contains a category to which the input record can be classified. Similarly, for regression problems, leaf node contains a numerical value to be mapped as a prediction for the given record.

6.4 Decision Tree Example

Let us look at an example decision tree used by an investment research analyst to choose the stocks to invest in. Please note that this is representative and not an actual investment approach.

The analyst has collected the historical data of 12 companies as depicted in the table below. Last column 'historical 1-year future returns >10%' is collected on a retrospective basis and acts as the label.

Table 26. Sample Data for Decision Trees

Revenue Growing for the last 5 years	P/E	Profitability Maintained for the last 5 years	Receivable days maintained for the last 5 years	Historical 1-year future returns > 10%
Y	20	Y	Y	Y
Y	18	Y	Y	Y
Y	18	Y	N	N
Y	14	Y	Y	Y
Y	19	Y	Y	Y
Y	14	N	Y	N
Y	8	Y	Y	Y
Y	28	Y	Y	N
Y	12	Y	Y	Y
N	10	Y	Y	N
Y	16	Y	Y	Y
Y	21	Y	Y	N

Now that we have the historical data, running a decision tree algorithm on the above data with the last column as the label gives us the below output.

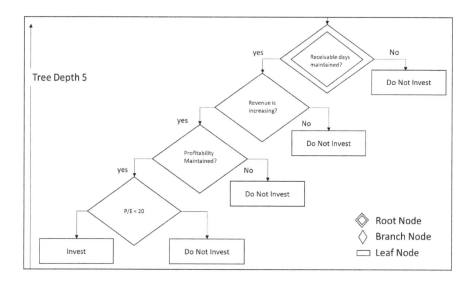

Figure 16. Generated Decision Tree

As you can see, the decision tree algorithm has been able to derive the key conditions from the given historical data for arriving at the investment decisions. Decisions are ordered in terms of priority, i.e. most important conditions are verified first to filter out fewer records for the next round of evolution. For example, the condition of 'Receivable days' seems to filter out maximum negative conditions, leaving fewer records for the next condition. Decision trees and decision tree based algorithms provide us a mechanism to construct such a sequence of questions/decision points to arrive at the expected outcome.

Some points to observe from the above example:

– Conditions at the root node and each branch node involve only a single feature like 'P/E <20.' Conditions at the nodes do not include multiple features.

– Conditions can be on categorical features like 'Revenue Growth' or 'Receivable Days' or numerical variables like P/E ratio. In case of numerical variables, the algorithm arrives at the actual split of the value at which the decision tree gives maximum predictability.

- In our example, the prediction of the decision tree is binary with possible outputs as 'Invest' or 'Do not Invest.' We can also build decision trees for a multi-class classification problem in which prediction value is one among several possible outcomes like 'high risk,' 'medium risk,' 'low risk' or 'safe.'

- Decision trees can also be built for regression problems in which the leaf node contains a numerical value as the prediction.

6.5   Decision Tree Algorithm

In building decision trees, the algorithm picks up the most important condition to split the data at the root node. This is done to give the maximum predictive power at the top of the tree and to form branches that are homogeneous. Following are the mathematical techniques used to arrive at a hierarchy of conditions.

Information Gain: This technique is used for classification problems in which label is one among the list of categories. We have seen the concepts of 'Entropy' and 'Information Gain' in the earlier section. Entropy is a mathematical measure of lack of information and hence a reduction in entropy is considered as information gain.

In table 27, we have sample data for 2 features 'Role' and 'Qualification' and the corresponding label 'Salary.' Let us see the baseline entropy of the label 'Salary' without considering any feature data.

Salary values are equally distributed among categories 'High,' 'Medium' and 'Low,' hence it is not possible to predict the salary without looking at the feature values. As label values are equally distributed among the 3 categories, it does not give us any predictive power and hence has zero information. Computed entropy in such a scenario is 1.

Table 27. Sample Data for Node Split

Role	Qualification	Salary
Manager	Graduate	High
Specialist	Graduate	Medium
Specialist	Post Graduate	Medium
Manager	Post Graduate	High
Line Staff	Post Graduate	Low
Line Staff	Graduate	Low

Now, the decision tree algorithm has 2 options to choose the feature variable for the root node condition. The node of a decision tree can only evaluate 1 condition involving 1 feature.

Table 28. Node Split Criteria

Split Option 1		Split Option 2	
Qualification	Salary	Role	Salary
Graduate	High	Manager	High
Graduate	Medium	Manager	High
Graduate	Low	Specialist	Medium
Post Graduate	High	Specialist	Medium
Post Graduate	Medium	Line Staff	Low
Post Graduate	Low	Line Staff	Low

Root node split based on the qualification, as seen in option 1, does not give us any additional information as the labels are equally distributed across qualification categories. We are not gaining any additional information as for both qualifications, salary values are equally distributed across 3 possible categories. However, root node split based on the role, as seen in option 2, gives us absolute information on the salary category as each split of the data maps only one salary category.

Salary values for all 'Manager' records are 'High' and so on. We are able to predict the salary based on the role without any ambiguity. Computed entropy for this split is significantly lower than baseline entropy and hence this split option gives us the maximum information gain. Once the condition for root node is selected, data is split into 2 branches based on that condition. Similar evaluation is done at each branch node level to split the data until we map all the training records to leaf nodes.

Residual Sum of Squares (RSS): This method is used in regression use cases with continuous numerical value as label to select the next most important condition for node split. RSS is a measure of variance of the given label data, which indicates the average distance to various data points from the mean. The algorithm selects the split condition that gives the maximum variance reduction among the split data. Let us consider the sample regression problem of predicting student marks based on the student background and hours studied.

Table 29. Sample Data for RSS

Background	Hours Spent	Marks
Urban	Below 40	50
Rural	Below 40	52
Urban	40–80	72
Rural	40–80	73
Urban	Above 80	88
Rural	Above 80	87

Similar to the earlier method, the decision tree algorithm has 2 options to split the data as represented in the table 30.

Table 30. Node Split Options

Split Option 1		Split Option 2	
Background	**Marks**	**Hours Spent**	**Marks**
Urban	50	Below 40	50
Urban	72	Below 40	52
Urban	88	40–80	72
Rural	52	40–80	73
Rural	73	Above 80	88
Rural	87	Above 80	87

As you can see from the above table, splits based on the background have high variance as marks across 'Urban' and 'Rural' categories are widely spread across. The split based on the 'Hours spent' has a very low variance among the 3 buckets 'Below 40,' '40–80' and 'Above 80.' Decision tree algorithm for regression chooses 'Hour Spent' as the condition for root node as this appears to reduce the RSS/variance significantly compared to the other option.

Based on the above techniques, the decision tree algorithm computes the information gain or RSS for each feature and possible values within that feature as conditions. Information gain or RSS is chosen depending on whether it is a classification or regression problem. The condition that reduces the RSS or gives maximum information gain is chosen as the split criteria. This process is recursively performed until the tree is fully grown or one of the termination conditions is reached.

We have seen that decision trees are intuitive and relatively easy to train but they have the twin problem of being unstable and incorrect. Decision trees are highly sensitive to the training data. Small changes in the training data can result in significant changes in the tree structure. Standalone decision trees have a problem in generalizing the model and have higher error rates on data that is not seen before. Ensemble methods using decision trees are used to achieve stable models that can generalize predictions.

6.6 Ensemble Methods

Ensemble methods rely on developing multiple trees from the training data and arriving at the prediction by aggregating the outcomes from different trees. This helps to improve the stability and accuracy of the models compared to that of a single decision tree. As we are aggregating the outputs of multiple decision trees, it smoothens the outcome, apart from stabilizing the model. Hence, for all practical use cases, ensemble methods based on decision trees are used instead of standalone trees.

We cannot simply run the decision tree algorithm on the same dataset to build multiple decision trees and form an ensemble as they all will be identical trees. There are different techniques to build multiple trees from the same given data and also to aggregate the outcomes from different trees to arrive at the prediction. Let us look at some of these techniques.

Bagging

Bagging technique creates multiple sets of training dataset from the given dataset by using a statistical sampling technique called bootstrapping. In this approach, records are selected randomly from the given dataset to be included in each training dataset. Let us say we have 'n' records in our training dataset. We will need 'm' sets of different training data to build that many decision trees in an ensemble. Each training set should be of the same size as the original training data with 'n' records.

For each of the 'm' target datasets, 'n' records are randomly selected from the input dataset with replacement. This means, even after we select a record from the input dataset randomly, it is still available for selection for the next record. All records are always available to be randomly picked as the next record. As we pick 'n' records randomly from the input dataset of 'n' records, this can result in some records being picked up multiple times and some not picked up at all. We repeat this 'm' times to create 'm' distinct datasets to train our ensemble of trees.

This technique ensures that we have 'm' number of trees grown from reasonably distinct datasets so that it can generalize the output.

Random Forest

Alternatively, we can build multiple trees from the same given dataset but randomly sub-select the features considered for building each node. In this, we will have 'm' identical datasets to build that many trees. We have seen earlier that the tree is grown from top-down and the algorithm looks for the feature and condition that gives the best possible split for the data records as the condition for the node. However, in random forest, at each node, a subset of features is randomly shortlisted among which the best possible condition to split the data is computed. Shortlisting features randomly at each node ensures that the trees grown are different from each other and hence the result is generalized well.

Boosting

Earlier ensemble techniques build multiple decision trees simultaneously and then aggregate the results of each tree to arrive at the prediction. Bagging looks at randomly selecting the data records whereas random forest looks to randomly sub-select features at each node. Boosting works by sequentially growing trees one after another in such a way that each tree builds upon the output of the previous tree. Boosting works on the principle of developing several simple models, also called as week learners, in a sequential manner so that when aggregated it gives a robust model/strong leaner.

Bagging and random forest methods look to build several trees which are complete/well grown and can give an independent prediction and then these are combined to form an ensemble. However, boosting looks at building simpler models in a sequential manner in such a way that each model addresses the gaps in the previous models.

Weightage for each tree is also computed at the time of building the tree based on the error rate of that tree for the training data. It can be mathematically proven that when such basic models are aggregated using computed weights, overall error is significantly reduced. Boosting is used in many practical applications.

7

Support Vector Machines

7.1 Introduction

Support vector machine is one of the popular machine learning techniques. In this chapter, we will discuss more on the functioning of support vector machine instead of the complex mathematics behind it. It is easy to understand support vector machine as a binary classifier and extend the understanding to multi-class classifiers and regression problems.

Let us say we have a training dataset with n-dimensional feature space and a binary label which can take positive or negative value. Support vector machine algorithm computes the decision boundary based on the training data that segregates the n-dimensional feature data into positive and negative cases. This decision boundary forms the solution and any future prediction can be made by computing which side of the boundary the new record falls into. Dimensions of the decision boundary depend on the number of features in the training dataset. A two-dimensional feature data is segregated by a single dimension decision boundary line between positive and negative cases. Similarly, a three-dimensional feature data is segregated by a two-dimensional plane between positive and negative cases.

Each feature in the training data corresponds to one dimension and the label adds the additional dimension. We can visualize up to three dimensions. For dimensions higher than 3, it is not possible to visualize them but underlying mathematical formulas work for higher dimensions as well. For example, training data for predicting the height of a child based on the height of both the parents has 2 features and 1 label. We can project this data as a three-dimensional chart, plotting the child's height based on the parents' heights for each record. Additional features like ethnicity or nutrition increase the number of dimensions and cannot be visualized in the form of charts.

In support vector machines for binary classification, two-dimensional feature data is segregated by a line, three-dimensional data is segregated by a plane whereas higher dimensional data is segregated by a multi-dimensional hyperplane. A solution hyperplane separates positive and negative use cases by the widest margin and hence is also called 'widest road method.' The median of such a wide road separating positive and negative cases forms the decision boundary. SVM algorithm uses the values of features and labels to arrive at the coordinates of such a hyperplane.

Fundamental Concepts: Some fundamental concepts to understand support vector machines better.

In mathematics, a line is represented by a formula:

$$Y = m\,x + C$$

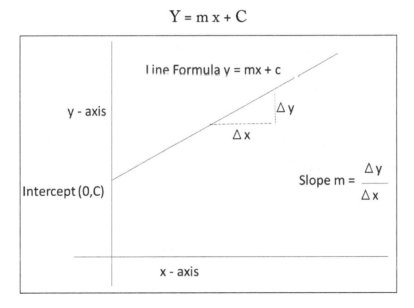

Figure 17. Mathematical Representation of a Line

This is a simple and straightforward formula from high-school mathematics. Value of y for a given point x depends on the slope and intercept represented by m and c respectively.

Rewriting the equation gives us a more general representation of the line:

$$ax + by + c = 0$$

In the above equation, the intercept and slope work out to be $- c/b$ and $- a/b$ respectively.

Two-dimensional data is visualized as a line in a two-dimensional chart and can be represented using a generic line equation:

$$ax + by + c = 0$$

Similarly, three-dimensional data is visualized as a plane in a three-dimensional chart and can be represented using a plane equation:

$$ax+ by + cz + d = 0$$

This representation can be extended to a hyperplane of any dimension.

Once we have the equation of a line, plane or hyperplane in the above format, we can find out the location of any given point with respect to that line, plane or hyperplane.

Let us take the line $ax + by + c = 0$ and a random point $(x1, y1)$, then we can find out if the point is on the line, above or below the line by substituting the point in the equation of the line.

$$Result = a * x1 + b * y1 + c$$

The point is exactly on the line if the result is zero. The point is above or below the line depending on whether the result is greater than or less than zero. The same logic can be applied for a two-dimensional plane or multi-dimensional hyperplane. Given a formula for a hyperplane and any random point, we can identify whether the point is on the plane, above or below it by substituting the values in the equation of the hyperplane. This feature is used for prediction for new records.

SVM algorithm derives the formula for a solution hyperplane which acts as the decision boundary between positive and negative cases. For the purpose of prediction for a new record, the position of that record compared to the decision boundary is computed as described above. Records which are above the decision boundary are marked as positive and those below the decision boundary are marked as negative.

7.2 SVM Example

Let us understand SVM with an example scenario in which we are trying to predict the Loan Approval status from the following features:

- Monthly Income

- Credit Score

We need to build an SVM to predict the Loan Eligibility as 'Approved' or 'Not Approved' based on the historical data of 100 records.

Now, we have the following scenario:

- We have 'm' samples (100 samples in this example)

- Each sample has 'n' features (2 features in this example, i.e. monthly income and credit score)

- Each label has 'p' categories (2 categories in this example, i.e. 'Approved,' 'Not Approved')

'n' features and 1 label represent 'n+1' dimensional data record. In our example, we have 2 features and 1 label and hence it is a three-dimensional data record. Sample data is presented in table 31.

Table 31. Sample Data for SVM

Income	Credit Score	Loan Approval
1000	750	Approved
300	650	Not Approved
2000	400	Approved
—	—	—

We have 2 categories of the label 'Loan Approval': 'Approved' and 'Not Approved.'

Each of the 100 records in the training dataset is mapped to one of the label categories. Each of these 100 records is a two-dimensional feature data (income, credit score) marked with one of the label categories, 'Approved' or 'Not Approved.'

Sample plot of the example is presented in figure 18.

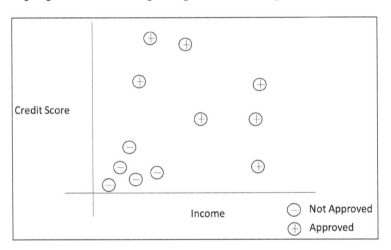

Figure 18. Loan Approval Status Plot

Support vector machine algorithm computes the formula for the hyperplane that most accurately separates the positive and negative data records. In our example, a line is computed that separates positive and negative samples by the widest margin possible. Once we compute the formula for such a hyperplane, it becomes the decision boundary for predicting future samples.

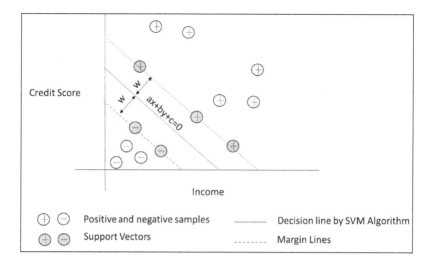

Figure 19. Decision Boundary for Loan Approval Status

In figure 19, line ax + by + c= 0 separates the positive and negative samples by the widest margin, represented as 2w. SVM algorithm computes a, b and c values in such a way that this line becomes the decision boundary for future predictions. Once the formula for such a hyperplane is available, the prediction for new records becomes very easy. We need to substitute the feature values of the new record (x1, y1) in the SVM computed hyperplane equation as below:

$$\text{Result of point } (x1, y1) = a * x1 + b * y1 + c$$

The given record is predicted as positive if the result of the above computation is greater than zero and negative if the result is less than zero.

A line separating 2 sets of data records by the widest margin is equidistant from the nearest points on either side of the line. In the above figure, we can see 2 dotted lines, one on each side of the decision line, at an equal distance of 'w,' called margin lines. As the algorithm looks for maximum margin, one or more training samples fall on each margin line. In other words, margin lines are extended until a point on either side falls on them and the center line between the margins forms the decision boundary.

So, we can say with certainty that a solution using the SVM algorithm has at least one or more data points falling exactly on the margin lines on either side. Data records (also referred to as feature vectors) that fall on either of the margin line are called support vectors. These are the points that are defining the solution for the widest margin problem, hence the name 'support vectors.' There can be several other points on the other side of the margin line which do not contribute to the solution as only the support vectors define the solution for the decision boundary.

Large Feature Space: We have looked at a two-dimensional feature dataset consisting of income and credit score for which the solution is a line separating the positive and negative points by the widest possible margin. But, in real-life use cases, we can have many more feature variables. Let us say our example has an additional feature, 'number of dependents,' apart from income and credit score. Our data is a three-dimensional feature space and our solution is a two-dimensional plane that separates positive and negative samples by the widest margin.

The solution for the three-dimensional feature space is a two-dimensional plane represented as ax + by + cz + d = 0.

Figure 20 gives the visual representation of such a solution.

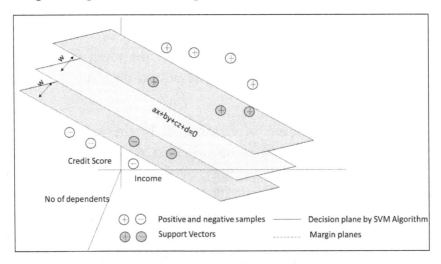

Figure 20. Two-Dimensional Decision Plane

The algorithm works with any number of dimensions even though we can visualize only up to a three-dimensional space. For example, an e-mail spam filter solution could consider each occurrence of a set of predefined words as a feature, resulting in hundreds of thousands of features. From each mail, the existence of these predefined words is extracted, which acts as a feature space for that mail. For 'n' dimensional feature set, we have 'n-1' dimensional solution that separates the positive cases from the negative ones.

7.3   Outliers and Noise – Soft Margin SVM

The example we have seen earlier is a very simple and ideal case, in which data is linearly separable and decision boundary can be computed using the SVM algorithms. SVM computes the margins in such a way that positive and negative records fall on either side of the margin lines with a decision boundary in between and at the center of the margin lines. Some training data records fall on the margin lines on both sides and are called 'support vectors.' This is also called hard margin SVM as no training data falls between the margin lines. But real-life scenarios are far from ideal. Presence of outliers and noise in the data can impact the outcome and hence the hard margin SVM algorithm needs to be enhanced to consider these aspects.

Outliers: Training data contains outliers and noise in most of the real-life use cases. We have seen that the SVM algorithm depends on a few training records called support vectors forming margin lines on either side of the decision boundary. Training samples away from the decision boundary do not contribute to the solution. The result of the SVM algorithm does not change even if we re-compute the decision boundary with only support vectors from the training samples, ignoring all the rest of the records.

The width of the road between the margin lines is an indication of the generalization capability of the model. A large gap between positive and negative margin lines indicates that the solution can accurately predict the outcome for unseen records, whereas a narrow gap means overfitting and higher error rate for unseen data. So, there is a significant influence of the support vectors on the solution and hence on the effectiveness of the predictions. The solution cannot generalize the predictions if the training data has outliers or noise impacting support vectors. Let us look at an example to see the impact of an outlier on the solution.

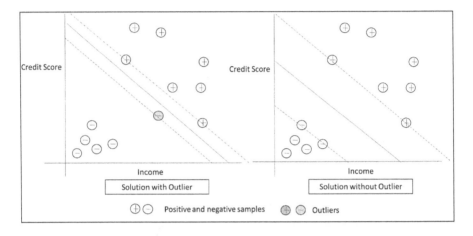

Figure 21. Impact of Outliers on SVM Decision Boundaries

In figure 21, the chart on the left-hand side has an outlier on the negative side which is pushing the solution very close to the positive cases. Such a solution is unlikely to perform well in prediction for new scenarios. The solution is heavily influenced by the presence of one outlier record as hard margin SVM does not allow any training records to be present between margin lines.

Noise: Noise in training data refers to erroneous samples in the training data. Records incorrectly classified in the training data can make it impossible for hard margin SVM algorithm to find a solution. Look at the example in figure 22.

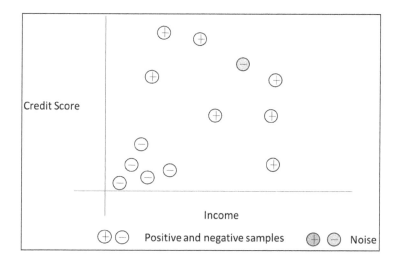

Figure 22. Noise in the Data Making it Linearly Inseparable

In the above figure, there is one record in the training data which is classified as negative but is well within the zone of positive cases. With such a noise in the training dataset, it is impossible for hard margin SVM algorithm to find a linearly separable line with positive and negative cases on either side.

Soft Margin SVM: Hard margin SVM algorithm ensures that all training data records satisfy the decision boundary and there is zero training error. This can lead to overfitting or less than optimum outcomes at the time of prediction for new records. Soft margin SVM is a superior alternative for real-life application of the SVM algorithm. Soft margin SVM introduces another parameter that allows for a trade-off between maximum margin and the error.

In hard margin SVM, we try to maximize the margin with all the positive and negative points complying with the solution. All support vectors are on the margin lines and the remaining training records are on either side of the margin. Hard margin SVM does not allow for any points to be present between the margin lines. However, in soft margin SVM, a loss/error term is introduced; it refers to the distance of the training points from their margin line. Loss/error term is only applicable for the records that fall on the wrong side of their respective margin lines. Negative or positive records on the correct side of the respective margin lines do not contribute to any loss. For a given solution of margin lines, total loss is computed as the sum of losses for each training data point. As you can see in figure 23, only the points which are on the wrong side of the margin contribute to the loss.

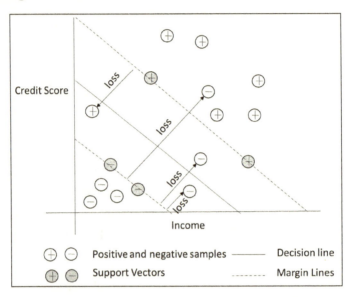

Figure 23. Soft Margin SVM

Hard margin SVM algorithm looks to maximize the margin in such a way that all the training data points fall on the correct side of the respective margin lines. Soft margin SVM algorithm also tries to maximize SVM but at the same time tries to minimize the total loss. Soft margin SVM algorithm could choose a wider margin as a trade-off for the loss/error introduced by one outlier or noise record which would end up of on the wrong side of the margin.

Soft margin SVM algorithm also provides a hyperparameter to balance this trade-off between the width of the margin and loss. This parameter specifies how much loss we are willing to tolerate for a wider margin. Lower the tolerance for error, the solution moves closer to the hard margin SVM. Higher tolerance for error will result in underfitting the training data, resulting in more training errors. This parameter needs to be tuned for the optimum balance between generalization and underfitting.

7.4 Non-Linear Models

Complex cause and effect relationships cannot be linearly separated. For example, rise in inflation is good for industry growth but beyond a certain point, it starts to negatively impact the growth. Such a relationship cannot be captured in a simple linearly separable decision boundary. Figure 24 represents an example of non-linear dependencies between features and label.

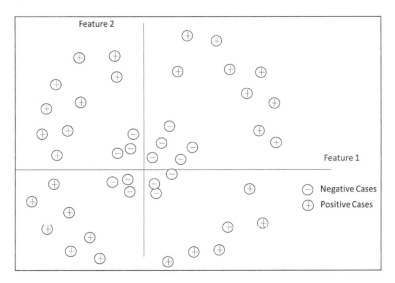

Figure 24. Data with Non-Linear Relationships

There is an obvious relationship between the training data points and the label, but it is not possible to separate the positive and negative labels using a straight line. In this example, training records which are closer to the origin with smaller feature values are negatively labeled whereas points with higher feature values are positively labeled.

One of the solutions for non-linear relationships is to increase the dimension of the training dataset and run the SVM algorithm on a higher dimensional dataset. In other words, additional dimensions to the training data improve the chances of linear separation using the SVM algorithm.

Let us convert our two-dimensional feature set in the above figure into a three-dimensional feature set that can be linearly separated by the SVM algorithm. Currently, we have 2 features: feature1 and feature 2. We can make it a three-dimensional feature set by adding a computed column, feature 3, in such a way that

$$\text{feature 3} = (\text{feature 1})^2 + (\text{feature 2})^2$$

With the inclusion of the computed feature, our training data set becomes a three-dimensional set with 3 features (feature 1, feature 2, feature 3) and the corresponding label.

Figure 25 indicates that by adding an additional dimension with an appropriate computed variable, the data becomes linearly separable. We have transformed the data so that it becomes linearly separable in the third dimension, introduced by adding a computed variable. We can perform the SVM algorithm on this higher dimensional dataset to compute the margins and decision boundary.

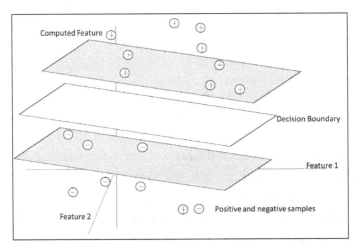

Figure 25. Feature Transformation to Help Linearly Separate Non-Linear Data Relationships

7.5 SVM Multi-Class Classification

So far, we have looked at SVM as a solution to find an optimum hyperplane that separates the positive and negative training samples. How do we extend this solution to problems where the output is not binary but one of the many possible classes? SVM algorithm can be used to cater to such multi-class problems. Let us look at some of the possible solutions.

Multi-Label, Binary Output: In a certain problem, we may need to attach more than one label for a record. For example, an image may be labeled with multiple categories like 'face,' 'group,' 'celebrity' and 'sky,' all at the same time. Such problems can be decomposed into multiple binary SVMs with each SVM computing one label such as whether the image contains a face or not. We need to build that many SVM classifiers as the number of possible labels which can be assigned to the record.

Single-Label, Multi-Class: In this kind of problems, each training record is assigned to one of the multiple possible categories. For example, in handwritten digit recognition, the image is tagged to one of the 10 values ranging from '0' to '9.' There are 2 widely used approaches to solve such problems using the SVM algorithm

One-vs-All: In this approach, a binary SVM is built for each label separately and trained using training data. Each SVM indicates whether the record belongs to the given category or not. In our example of handwritten digit recognition, we build 10 SVMs trained using the same data. Each of the 10 SVMs represents a digit from '0' to '9.' SVM for digit '0' computes a hyperplane that separates '0' training samples from the rest of the samples. Similarly, SVMs for other digits compute the hyperplanes for their respective labels.

At the time of prediction for a new record, it is processed in all the SVMs to arrive at the result. It is possible that one record may be shown as positive in more than one SVM. In such cases, distance from the decision boundary is taken as a measure to find the correct label. Distance from the boundary is a measure of confidence on the selected label. Table 32 contains the example result from the set of SVMs and corresponding prediction.

Table 32. SVM Multi-Class: One vs. All

SVM Machine	Result	Distance from Decision Boundary	Prediction
0	Negative	NA	We have 6 SVMs giving negative results. Out of the remaining 4, SVM for label '8' has produced the result which has the maximum distance from the decision boundary. Hence, the image of the handwritten digit can be labeled as 8.
1	Negative	NA	
2	Negative	NA	
3	Positive	1.5	
4	Negative	NA	
5	Negative	NA	
6	Positive	.5	
7	Negative	NA	
8	Positive	4	
9	Positive	.5	

One-vs-One: In this approach, several binary SVMs are built for pairs of labels using a subset of training data. For example, an SVM is created for labels '0' and '1' and is trained using the '0' and '1' labeled records from the overall training data. As we are building an SVM for every combination of label values, this can result in a large number of SVMs depending on the number of output categories. However, each SVM is trained with a subset of the overall training data. For a problem with 'n' output categories, we need to build 'factorial n-1' SVMs. For a 10-digit classification, we need 45 binary classifiers representing each combination of digits.

At the time of prediction, each record is evaluated by all the SVMs to categorize the records between the 2 labels. The label which gets maximum votes from the array of SVMs is selected as the label. Table 33 contains sample results of 45 SVMs created for each combination of digits. Each cell in the table represents the result of the prediction using an SVM classifier for that row-column combination of digits.

Table 33. SVM Multi-Class: One vs. One

SVM Pairs/ inference	0	1	2	3	4	5	6	7	8	9
0	NA	0	2	3	0	5	0	7	0	9
1		NA	1	1	4	5	1	7	1	9
2			NA	2	2	5	2	2	8	9
3				NA	3	5	3	3	8	9
4					NA	5	6	4	8	4
5						NA	5	5	8	5
6							NA	6	6	6
7								NA	7	7
8									NA	9
9										NA

Aggregating the prediction outputs of all 45 SVMs gives the following result.

Table 34. SVM Multi-Class – One vs. One – Inference

Digit	0	1	2	3	4	5	6	7	8	9
Count	4	4	5	4	3	8	4	4	4	5

So, from the above table, digit '5' has the maximum number of predictions compared to other categories and can be taken as the final prediction.

7.6 Support Vector Regression

Support vector algorithm and its basic principles can also be used for regression problems. In case of classification, we find the optimum hyperplane that segregates the positive and negative samples by the widest margin. For a two-dimensional feature space, we have a line as the decision boundary that classifies positive and negative cases. In regression, we have to predict a real number as the output. For a two-dimensional feature space, the regression algorithm computes a plane that explains the training output within a small error range.

For a given data record of 2 features, the corresponding point on the solution plane gives the prediction. For an 'n' dimensional feature set, support vector classification results in an 'n-1' dimensional hyperplane whereas regression results in an 'n' dimensional solution hyperplane for prediction. For classification problems, the computed hyperplane acts as the decision boundary whereas for regression problems, the hyperplane provides the prediction. Support vector regression supports all the key features of the classification machine.

Outliers and Noise: Due to noise and outliers in the data, it may not be possible to find an optimum hyperplane within the acceptable range. In this case, an error term is introduced to cater to such data points and the algorithm is optimized to balance between overfitting and over-generalizing. Overfitting results in memorizing data whereas over-generalizing results in higher training error.

Non-linear Regression: Similar to non-linear classification, non-linear regression can be performed by artificially increasing the number of dimensions in the feature data. This is achieved by adding computed variables in such a way that the results converge on a hyperplane. Such a transformed feature space is able to capture the non-linear relationships in the original dimensions.

7.7 SVM Algorithm and Kernel Trick

So far, we have looked at the functioning of the SVM algorithm. The algorithm takes the training records and computes an optimum hyperplane that separates positive labeled records from the negative ones.

This hyperplane acts as the decision boundary for future predictions. New records are labeled as positive or negative depending on which side of the hyperplane they are placed.

But how does the SVM algorithm compute such a hyperplane? We will only have a brief look at the algorithm as the underlying mathematical formulas are quite complex.

SVM Algorithm: SVM algorithm has to find the hyperplane that meets the following objectives for all the given training records:

- Maximize the distance between the solution hyperplane and margin lines on either side. This is the optimization problem to select the widest road separating positive and negative labels.

- All the training records with a positive label should be on or above the positive margin plane. Similarly, all records with a negative label should be on or below the negative margin plane. This constraint is placed on each and every training record. We have that many constraints as the number of training records.

We have the problem of maximizing the distance between the margin lines with a constraint that each and every training record lies on either side of the respective margin lines depending on their label. This is also referred to as 'constrained optimization problem.'

This constrained optimization problem is converted into a maximization problem using Lagrangian multiplier formulas. This approach has the following advantages:

- The original constrained optimization problem is converted into a convex problem. There is one global solution and it does not encounter local minima.

- Lagrangian multipliers are computed for each training record but the results are sparse. Only those training records that are lying on the margin lines (support vectors) have positive values and all other records have zero values. This makes it computationally simple to arrive at the prediction.

- This formula is structured in the form of scalar product multiplication between different training records. This is a useful feature in scaling the data to higher dimensions using Kernel Trick.

The solution for Lagrangian representation can be found by several techniques like gradient ascent or sequential minimum optimization.

Kernel Trick: Lagrangian representation structures the problem in the form of a scalar product between different training records. SVM algorithm requires computation of scalar product of every possible combination of the training dataset. For a training set consisting of 100 records, the SVM algorithm requires computation of 100 x 100 dot products between each possible combination of input feature records.

In many cases, training data in the original feature space may not be linearly separable and needs to be enhanced by inducing additional dimensions in the feature space. For example, input data can be enhanced to include a square of each variable additionally, thus doubling the number of features. It can be computationally expensive to induce additional dimensions in the feature space for large training datasets and compute scalar products between those higher dimensional records.

Kernel trick is used to achieve higher dimensionality in the original feature space without actually transforming the data. The trick is to apply the transformation to increase the feature space after the computation of scalar product between the pair of records. The kernel function is applied on the scalar product between the 2 training records, in contrast to applying the transformation in the original feature space and computing the scalar product. Both approaches produce the same result but using the kernel trick requires significantly less processing. Polynomial and Radial Basis Kernels are the 2 most commonly used functions for transforming data into higher dimensions.

8

Bayesian Learning

8.1 Introduction

Bayesian learning is a simple yet very effective machine learning technique. It is based on the Bayesian theorem of probabilities. Let us look at some of the fundamentals to understand the algorithm.

Probability: Probability is the foundation of statistics and indicates the chances of a particular event occurring. Probability computed on a well-collected data sample gives us a fairly good extrapolation of the real-world events. The number of records observed to arrive at the probability is referred to as sample size. Baseline data/Sample data contains the records using which the probability of any event is arrived at. Let us look at the following data sample for a marathon runner's schedule consisting of 10 records of each 2 attributes.

Table 35. Sample Data for Probability

Sample	Raining?	Running?
Day 1	No	No
Day 2	Yes	No
Day 3	No	Yes
Day 4	No	No
Day 5	Yes	No
Day 6	No	Yes
Day 7	Yes	No
Day 8	No	Yes
Day 9	Yes	No
Day 10	Yes	Yes

From the given sample, the probability of raining is 0.5 as it was raining in 5 out of total 10 days in the sample dataset. Similarly, the probability of running is 0.4 as the runner was practicing on 4 out of 10 days.

Conditional Probability: Conditional probability is about a particular event 'A' occurring given that another event 'B' occurred. For example, the probability of rain when the athlete goes running is a conditional probability. Here, we have 2 events and their independent probabilities. We have the probability of rain (0.5) and the probability of running (0.4) based on the overall sample data of 10 records. However, conditional probability is only based on the subset of sample data that matches the given condition.

To compute the probability of rain when the athlete goes running, we subset the sample data to only those records/dates in which the athlete has run. The probability of rain is computed on this subset of data and not the entire sample data. To compute the probability of rain when the athlete goes running, let us subset the data to those records in which the athlete is running.

Table 36. Subset of Data for Conditional Probability

Sample	Raining?	Running?
Day 3	No	Yes
Day 6	No	Yes
Day 8	No	Yes
Day 10	Yes	Yes

We have 4 records out of which it was raining on only 1 day. So, the conditional probability of raining when the athlete was running is 0.25, i.e. 1 in 4 records.

Conditional probability is not commutative, i.e. probability of A occurring given B is not the same as probability of B occurring given A. In the first case, we subset the sample space to those records that match the condition B whereas in the latter case, we subset the records to those that match condition A. Let us look at the probability of the athlete running when it was raining. We need to subset the data to those records in which rain was recorded.

Table 37. Subset of Data for Conditional Probability

Sample	Raining?	Running?
Day 2	Yes	No
Day 5	Yes	No
Day 7	Yes	No
Day 9	Yes	No
Day 10	Yes	Yes

We have 5 records in which rain is marked as 'Yes' out of which 1 record was marked for running. So, the probability of the athlete running when it was raining was 0.2, i.e. 1 in 5 records.

Combined Probability: Combined probability is the probability of 2 events occurring together in the sample space. In the above example, the probability of rain and the athlete running on any given day is the combined probability. Unlike conditional probability, combined probability is based on the total sample size and not on a subset. Simple logic tells us that combined probability is always less than the individual probabilities. Combined probability is also commutative, which means combined probability of A and B is the same as combined probability of B an A. As we are looking for the occurrence of both the events in a sample space, the order does not matter.

In our example, the probability of raining and the athlete running is 0.1 as there is only 1 record in the entire sample space in which both are registered as 'Yes.'

Table 38. Subset of Data for Combined Probability

Sample	Raining?	Running?
Day 10	Yes	Yes

Combined probability can be computed using the below formula which is intuitive to understand:

Combined probability (A, B) = Probability (A) * Conditional probability of (B|A)

Probability of A multiplied by conditional probability of B when A occurs gives us the combined probability of those 2 events occurring together.

Independence of Events: Combined probability is the simple product of the individual probabilities of the events A and B, provided these events are completely independent of each other. This is really simple to prove as the conditional probability of a condition B given A is the same as the probability of B if these events are completely independent. As the occurrence of condition A does not impact B, it is expected that the probability of B is going be the same across the entire sample set as it is for the subset of data matching condition A.

For fully independent A and B,

- Conditional probability of (B|A) = Probability (B), hence

- Combined probability (A, B) = Probability (A) * Probability (B)

The concept of independence of events is very important and is used effectively in the naive Bayes algorithm to solve many practical problems.

8.2   Bayesian Theorem

Bayesian theorem provides a mathematical formula to compute the conditional probability of an event A given the condition B (represented as A|B), provided we have the individual probabilities of A and B separately, as well as conditional probability of B given A (represented as B|A).

The formula itself is very simple and easy to compute. But what is the relevance of Bayes theorem in machine learning? How do we use Bayes theorem in machine learning?

In supervised machine learning problems, we have the training data with several features and the corresponding label. We are expected to learn the relationship between these variables using the machine learning algorithm. Once we learn these dependencies, we need to be able to predict the outcome/label for any data in the future. Let us rephrase this problem and define it as:

– The algorithm to find out the conditional probabilities for each category of output label for a given input record with several feature variables.

Once we have the conditional probabilities for each category of the label, then we can choose the category with the highest probability as the prediction of the model. Bayesian learning works based on this principle of computing conditional probabilities of label categories for the given combination of feature values. For this, we need to compute

– Conditional Probability for each category of Label|Given Combination of Features

As per Bayes theorem, we can compute the above values, provided we have:

– Probability of Label (for each category)

– Probability of Feature (for each category)

– Conditional Probability of (each feature|for each category of label)

We have the training dataset with features and label from which above probabilities can be derived. As part of training the Bayesian model, the above values are computed from the training data. Once we have the trained model, given a new record we can compute the conditional probabilities for all output categories and choose the one with the highest probability.

Let us take an example data with 1 feature (Employment Status) and 1 label (Loan Eligibility), both of which are categorical in nature.

Table 39. Structure of Sample Data

Employment Status	Loan Eligibility
Employed	Yes
Self-Employed	No
Unemployed	

We need to predict the Loan Eligibility for the given employment status. To restate the problem in Bayesian learning, we need to:

- Compute Conditional Probability of Loan Eligibility 'Yes' for the given employment status

- Compute Conditional Probability of Loan Eligibility 'No' for the given employment status

We can compare the above 2 probabilities and choose the one with the higher value as the prediction.

As part of training the model, the algorithm computes the following values which will be used for the above prediction:

- Probability of employment status 'Employed'

- Probability of employment status 'Self-Employed'

- Probability of employment status 'Unemployed'

- Probability of Loan Eligibility 'Yes'

- Probability of Loan Eligibility 'No'

- Conditional Probability of 'Employed'|Loan Eligibility 'Yes'

- Conditional Probability of 'Self-Employed'|Loan Eligibility 'Yes'

- Conditional Probability of 'Unemployed'|Loan Eligibility 'Yes'

- Conditional Probability of 'Employed'|Loan Eligibility 'No'

- Conditional Probability of 'Self-Employed'|Loan Eligibility 'No'

- Conditional Probability of 'Unemployed'|Loan Eligibility 'No'

These values can be used to compute the prediction for any future data using the Bayesian formula to arrive at the prediction.

8.3   Naive Bayes Algorithm

In the above example, we have assumed that there is only one feature variable. But practical use cases have a large number of features as part of the training dataset. So, our single feature problem statement

- Conditional probability of label|feature

Becomes

- Conditional probability of label|feature 1, feature 2, …feature n

To be able to compute this at the time of prediction, we need to compute the inverse conditional probability at the time of training, i.e.

- Conditional probability of feature 1, feature 2, …feature n|label

Each categorical feature can take multiple values. Feature column 'Employment Status' in the previous example can take 1 of the possible 3 values. As part of training, we need to compute the probability of each combination of features for the given label value. For datasets with a large number of feature variables with each having a number of categories, this can be computationally very intensive to calculate the probabilities for various combinations. Also, we may not have enough data records for each combination of features and label categories to compute the probabilities as part of training. Naive Bayes comes to rescue here.

Naive Bayes algorithm assumes that all the feature variables are independent of each other, which greatly simplifies our above problem. We have derived at the beginning of this chapter that the combined probability becomes a product of individual probabilities provided the events are independent.

With this assumption of independence between feature variables

- Conditional probability of (feature 1, feature 2…feature n| label) becomes

- Conditional probability of (feature 1| label) * Conditional probability of (feature 2| label) …* Conditional probability of (feature n| label)

It is nothing but a simple multiplication of probabilities of each feature value for a given label. This is much easier to compute and proven to be very effective. As this algorithm assumes independence of feature variables, it is called naive Bayes.

Naive Bayes algorithm greatly simplifies the computationally intensive solution by assuming independence of features. This has proved to be very effective in text classification and natural language processing problems.

9

K-Means Clustering

9.1 Introduction

K-means is an unsupervised algorithm to identify clusters within the training data, without the need for labeling them for training. K-means is an iterative process to identify clusters of data within a large dataset. It arrives at a predefined number of groups from the given data, based on the distance between them in multi-dimensional space. Conceptually, K-means is very simple and can generate additional insights into the data. Let us look at K-means with an example.

Table 40. Sample Data for K-Means

Individual	Age	Expense/ Income%	Individual	Age	Expense/ Income%
A1	20	80	A11	30	60
A2	45	55	A12	80	90
A3	35	50	A13	55	50
A4	38	45	A14	40	45
A5	50	60	A15	43	50
A6	60	70	A16	24	75
A7	25	75	A17	31	55
A8	42	50	A18	65	70
A9	75	80	A19	48	50
A10	28	65	A20	70	75

Just by looking at the data, we cannot interpret much. Thankfully, data is 2 dimensional, so we can plot it on a scatter plot, which gives slightly better insights than looking at the data.

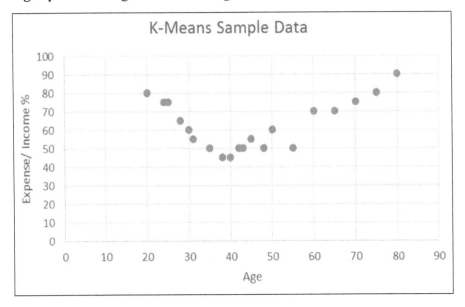

Figure 26. K-Means Sample Data

Now, K-means can help in clustering the individuals into several groups. Let us say we want to group the data into 3 buckets so that we can target the bucket with maximum potential for selling savings products.

9.2   K-Means Algorithm

K-means work with iterative logic.

Step 1: Randomly choose 'n' records from the data where 'n' is a number of clusters we want to create from the data. In our example, we want to group the data into 3 clusters. These randomly chosen records are temporary centroids (also called mean) of the clusters.

Step 2: Algorithm associates every other data record in the input to 1 of the 3 clusters based on the proximity to the centroid. In other words, each record is mapped to the closest cluster. At the end of this step, we have all the records mapped to 'n' clusters.

Step 3: For each cluster, a new centroid is computed in such a way that it is at the center of the data records in that cluster. At the end of step 3, we have 3 means which are at the center of their clusters.

Step 4: Algorithm can be repeated from step 2 until satisfactory results are achieved. Iterations are stopped when bucketing of input records is stabilized with no/negligible movement of records across clusters.

Figure 27 depicts the clusters arrived at by the algorithm.

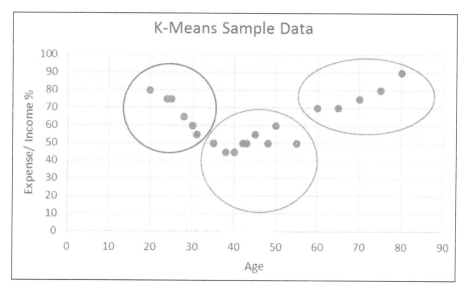

Figure 27. K-Means Clusters

As you can see in the figure above, we have 3 clusters of data automatically generated by the system. Even though our example shows two-dimensional data, the algorithm works well for higher dimensional data as well. However, the K-mean algorithm cannot label these clusters. Records are grouped into clusters based on the distance between them in higher dimensional space but no interpretation for the clustering can be given by the algorithm. Domain knowledge is required to analyze the clusters and interpret the meaning as well as to appropriately use the information.

Let us analyze our sample clusters.

Left Cluster – Young and High Expense Group: This group seems to have higher expenses as a percentage of income. This may be because of low income or lack of financial awareness, resulting in high expenses or both.

Middle Cluster – Middle Age and Low Expense Group: This group seems to have a lower ratio of expenses. This can be the result of increased income as well as awareness of savings due to increased responsibilities.

Right Cluster – Old age and High Expense Group: This group seems to have higher expenses. This may be due to reduced income levels post-retirement or reduced need to save as financial responsibilities are fulfilled.

So, for a bank looking to target savings products, they can look at the Middle cluster as this group of individuals has the maximum potential and intention to save. This example and analysis are for illustration only.

10

Neural Networks

10.1 Overview

Neural networks are a machine learning technique modeled based on the way the human brain is structured. The comparison with the brain and related terminology is a bit superficial but helps greatly in understanding the functioning of neural networks. The human brain develops over a period based on the experiences, learning patterns and circumstances. Billions of neurons and their interconnections form the basis for intelligence/knowledge/experience of the human. Neurons and their connections that store human knowledge, experiences and memories process various inputs received through sensory organs and provide appropriate responses.

Inputs perceived from sensory organs like eye, nose, ear, tongue and skin activate a set of neurons in the brain, generating brain response and communicating the same as instructions to different body parts. At the time of learning a new skill like swimming or driving, initially one struggles to make coordinated moves between different body parts. Once learned and practiced enough, people can swim or drive effortlessly without applying their conscious mind. This can be seen as an effect of activating and establishing new connections between the neurons during the learning phase. Once these grooves are established, it becomes effortless for the brain to pass on necessary instructions for coordinated movements.

Human-built neural networks function based on the same principle but are much less sophisticated than the human brain. These networks are less dense and less capable than the human brain in many aspects.

10.2   Neural Networks – How Do They Learn?

Neural networks are the foundation of deep learning and many recent advancements in machine learning. Neural networks are a machine learning technique to extract the relationship between pairs of input and output records given in the training dataset.

Let us look at the plain English explanation of neural networks here before diving deep into the details.

Neural networks are user-defined nested mathematical functions with several user induced variables which can be modified in a systematic trial and error basis to arrive at the closest mathematical relationship between given pairs of inputs and outputs.

Let's look at each term closely.

User-Defined: Neural networks operate under the premise that there exists a mathematical function between a given set of inputs and outputs. Neural networks algorithm tries to arrive at the best suited computational model for the given data. Neural network designers need to specify the mathematical function to represent the relationship between inputs and outputs. The mathematical function defined initially can be tuned based on the training results. Such a mathematical function contains a number of user induced variables also called trainable parameters or weights.

Nested: To represent the complexity of the relationship between training inputs and outputs, mathematical functions can be designed in a nested manner. The design may include several layers of mathematical functions with outputs of one layer of function feeds in as input to the next layer of mathematical function. Example of 2 layered mathematical model with f1() as the first layer nested within the second layer function f2():

Output = f2 (f1(Weight Set1, inputs), f1(Weight Set 2, inputs), f1(Weight Set 3, inputs), Weight Set 4)

Mathematical Functions: Each layer of mathematical function has 2 components:

- Aggregation Function: Inputs to the function are weighted with user induced variables to compute the weighted sum.

- Activation Function: Weighted sum is passed through an activation function to introduce non-linearity in the model. Mathematical models built with nested non-linear functions can better capture the complex relationships hidden in the data.

Mathematical functions used in neural networks are continuous and hence differentiable. This means it is possible to compute the change in the output of the function for a small change in the value of each of the user induced variables. Change in the output of the mathematical model for a small change in the induced variable is usually referred to as the output gradient of that variable.

User Induced Variables (Trainable Parameters): All inputs to mathematical functions are weighted by user induced variables to arrive at the weighted sum. User induced variables are the only modifiable parameters in training, as inputs/outputs and the model are fixed. User induced variables are modified during training so that the model takes the training input and produces the output as close to the training output as possible. User induced variables are also referred to as weight matrix.

Trial and Error: User induced variables in the model are adjusted on a trial and error basis so that for all the training inputs, it produces the output closer to the given output. Initially, the model output is computed using initialized variables. Cost function represents the difference between computed output and expected output of the model. User induced variables are adjusted to slightly reduce the cost in each learning step. This is done in small steps over several iterations. Linear algebra/differentiation techniques are used to find the change required in each of the variables to reduce the cost, which is also called cost function gradient for these variables.

Systematic: In case the user-defined mathematical formula is not able to map the inputs and outputs for any combination of user induced variables, then different variations of mathematical formulas and training methods are used systematically.

Closest Mathematical Relationship: Once we arrive at the right values for the user induced variables, the model can be considered as trained and ready. For such values of user induced variables, the computed output of the model for all given inputs is within the tolerable limits. This model is ready to process any future inputs and produce a prediction.

So far, we have looked at the intuitive meaning of neural networks and their learning. In practice, neural networks are represented in the form of layers of neurons. Figure 28 depicts the typical representation of neural networks.

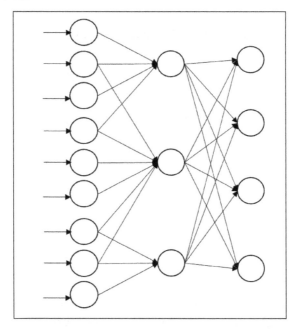

Figure 28. Neural Networks Representation

Each neuron is a combination of aggregation and activation mathematical functions. The first layer of neurons accepts inputs and the last layer of neurons produces output. There can be one or more hidden layers between input and output layers. Each hidden layer of neurons represents another layer of mathematical formulas organized in a nested manner. In a fully connected feedforward network, each neuron in a layer is connected to each and every neuron in the next layer. Neurons in the input layer are connected to all the neurons in the first hidden layer and neurons in the first hidden layer are connected to all the neurons in the next layer, which can be a hidden or output layer.

Each neuron has a trainable variable called bias and each connection between neurons has a trainable variable called weight. These are user induced trainable parameters in the neural network mathematical formula. Combination of weights and biases in a neural network is referred to as weight matrix. As the training data flows from input to output layer, it gets transformed by mathematical functions based on the values of the weight matrix. Training a neural network is about finding the right combination of values for the weight matrix in such a way that network output is as close to the actual output as possible.

In a trained network, entire knowledge is stored within the weight matrix data structure. Entire knowledge can be replicated by copying this data structure to any machine along with the network design. Once trained, it is very simple to generate a prediction from neural networks by simply navigating the input through the layers of mathematical functions using the weight matrix. The prediction process is not computation intensive and does not need significant resources. Let us look at an example of a data structure to store weight matrix.

As depicted in figure 29, we have a fully connected feedforward neural network with the following features:

- Training input record has 100 features, resulting in 100 input neurons

- Has a hidden layer of 20 neurons

- Has the output layer of 10 neurons; each output neuron indicates a category of output

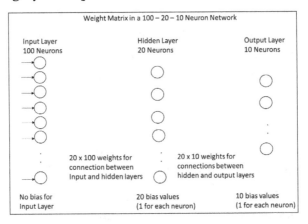

Figure 29. Weight Matrix in a Neural Network – Example

Here is the data structure for the weight matrix for the above design:

- 2000 weights for connections between 100 input neurons and 20 hidden layer neurons

- 20 biases for 20 neurons in the hidden layer

- 200 weights for connections between 20 hidden layer neurons and 10 output neurons

- 10 biases for 10 neurons in the output layer

- No bias values defined for the input layer as these neurons take input feeds directly

This gives us the total of 2230 variables in the weight matrix out of which 2200 are weights and 30 are bias variables. Training starts with randomly initialized weights (or using a superior initialization algorithm). These weights and biases are adjusted as part of the training.

10.3   Components of a Neural Network

Let us unpack the neural networks by having a deeper look at the components in it. We cannot understand the significance of the whole without knowing its parts. We cannot comprehend the parts without knowing their relevance in the big picture. So, we will initially introduce the components of the neural network, then go on to learn in detail about how neural networks learn and function. In the next chapter, which focuses on neural networks design, we will come back to discuss the significance of each component in neural networks design.

Figure 30 gives an overview of all the components in a single hidden layer neural network.

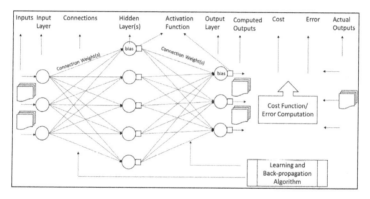

Figure 30. Components of a Neural Network

Input Layer: Neural networks are organized in the form of layers of neurons. The first layer in the neural network is always the input layer. The first layer should have that many neurons as the number of feature variables in the training dataset. Input data features are mapped to the neurons in the input layer.

Output Layer: The last layer in the neural networks is always the output layer. The number of output neurons depends on the way we design the neural network for the given problem. For regression problems, it is typically one output neuron, assuming we are building the model for one label. For classification problems, the number of output neurons should be the number of possible classes for the label. For example, a handwritten digit classification problem will have 10 possible output classes and hence 10 output neurons indicating each possible output.

Hidden layers: Hidden layers are in between input and output layers. Each hidden layer has a set of neurons connected with neurons in adjacent layers and an activation function for non-linearity. The number of neurons in the input and output layer is determined by the training data. However, neurons in the hidden layer are a design aspect of the solution. Neural network design has to address the following questions:

– How many hidden layers are needed?

– How many neurons in each hidden layer?

– How are the neurons in the hidden layer connected to adjacent layers?

These design choices must be made after careful consideration of several factors including nature of the problem, number of training data records and other network parameters.

Connections: Neural network is a directed graph with each layer of neurons connected to the next layer of neurons. Weight matrix consists of weights of connections between these neurons and these are optimized as part of training to minimize the error of the network for the given training data.

Fully Connected Feedforward Network: In a fully connected feedforward network, all the neurons in each layer, except the output layer, are connected to all the neurons in the next layer. All the neurons in the input layer are connected to all the neurons in the first hidden layer, which are further connected to the next hidden layer and so on. Finally, all neurons in the last hidden layer are connected to the output neurons. Basic neural networks are fully connected whereas deep learning neural networks have advanced architecture for connections between the layers. We will discuss these in detail in the deep learning section of the book.

Weighted Input: Neurons in all the layers (except the input layer) receive incoming connections from neurons in the previous layer. In a fully connected layer, each neuron receives inputs from each and every neuron in the previous layer. These inputs are weighted according to the weight of the connections between them. As the weights are modified by the learning algorithm, weighted inputs received by a neuron change accordingly. This will help in adjusting the weights in such a way that the computed output is as close to the expected output as possible.

Bias: Bias is the trainable parameter captured for each neuron in the network except for the neurons in the input layer. Neurons in the input layer receive the training inputs and connect them with the hidden layer directly and hence no bias is needed at this layer.

Activation Function: Neurons in our brain are activated based on the inputs received from sensory organs. Different neurons get triggered for different events and an appropriate response is formulated in the brain. Similarly, neurons in the neural network are triggered depending on the inputs passed on to them. A mathematical function called 'activation function' is defined for each layer of neurons and all the neurons within the same layer have the same activation function.

Typically, a layer of neurons is named after their activation function like sigmoid layer, tanh layer or softmax layer. In a neural network, different layers can have different activation functions. Selection of an appropriate activation function is a key decision of neural network design. Activation function computes the output of a neuron based on the weighed inputs received from the neurons in previous layers. Non-linear activation function transforms the weighted inputs in such a way that changes in the weighted inputs and corresponding changes in the output are not linearly correlated. This helps in capturing complex relationships between inputs and outputs in the training data.

Some of the activation functions are described below.

- **Perceptron**: Perceptron is a linear predictor function that produces the output 0 if the weighted input is less than a certain threshold defined at each neuron level called bias. Perceptron returns 1 if the weighted input is greater than the bias. Weights and bias are trainable parameters changed by the learning algorithm to arrive at the optimum output. Perceptrons are not very amenable to training, as their output is not a smooth curve.

- **Linear Activation**: Linear activation for a neuron simply passes on the input as output without any transformation. Linear activation is typically used in the output layer of regression problems.

- **Sigmoid**: Sigmoid function adds non-linearity to the network. Sigmoid activation function produces an output value between 0 and 1 for any given range of weighted inputs. For the weighted input values closer to negative infinity, the sigmoid value approaches 0. For the values closer to positive infinity, the sigmoid produces 1 as the output.

- **Tanh**: Tanh is a non-linear activation function similar to sigmoid. Tanh mathematical function can take the weighted input values from – Infinity to + Infinity and produce an output ranging from −1 and 1 compared to the output range of 0 to 1 for sigmoid.

- **Rectified Linear Unit (ReLU)**: ReLU produces linear output for all positive values of weighted input whereas outputs '0' for all negative values of weighted inputs. For all positive weighted values, the input is passed as output directly. ReLU is useful in addressing the vanishing gradient problem in deep neural networks, which we will discuss later.

- **Softmax**: In all the activation functions we have seen so far, the output of a neuron depends on its weighted input. However, in softmax, the output of a neuron is not only dependent on its inputs but also depends on the inputs of other neurons in the same layer. Softmax activation works in such a way that the sum of outputs across all neurons is 1. So, when there is an increase in the output of one neuron, there is an equivalent reduction in the outputs of the remaining neurons. Softmax is well suited in classification problems as it produces probabilistic distribution across output categories.

Error: Error is the difference between the expected output and the actual output produced by the neural network. For example, in a neural network designed for the classification of digits, the error reflects the ratio of digits classified incorrectly from the training data. Error in the model is specific to use case. Error of a regression model predicting holiday season sales indicates the difference between actual sales and predicted sales.

Cost Function: Neural networks learn by the trial and error approach to reduce the error of the network. The error of a neural network is the difference between expected output and predicted output for all the training records. For example, in image recognition use cases, number of images incorrectly classified represents the error of the model. However, the error may not be amenable to training, as it is not a smooth function of the trainable weights of the neural network. For the learning to be efficient, we need it to be slow and incremental. We need such a function to be continuous and differentiable with the weight matrix.

Cost function is a mathematical function that is proxy to the error of the neural network. Cost function is continuous, smooth and very much amenable to training. For example, the number of records incorrectly predicted by the neural network is considered an error, but the cost can be the quadratic difference between the computed and expected output of the neurons, as it is more amenable to differentiation and training.

Cost function is at the heart of the training. Cost is minimized by optimizing the weight matrix during training. In simple terms, the cost function is a mathematical expression that indicates the amount by which the computed value of the neural network differs from the historical value. Following important points must be noted:

- Cost function should be proxy to the error. Error in the model should come down as the cost is reduced during training.

- Cost function should be amenable to training. It should be possible to express cost function in terms of expected and actual output of neurons. Such a direct representation can help modify the weight matrix to get the desired outputs.

- Cost function needs to be smooth. Cost function should be specified in such a way that small changes in the weight matrix result in small changes in the cost.

- Cost function is applicable only for the outputs generated by the output layer. Cost function is not applicable for input or hidden layers.

We will revisit the cost function for better understanding in the next chapter.

Learning and Back-Propagation Algorithm: Training a neural network is an optimization problem. We have many components in the neural network:

Fixed Parameters: Like number of layers, number of neurons in each layer, activation function and cost function. Values for these fixed components are finalized as part of the network design.

Trainable Parameters: Also called weight matrix, which determines the output of the network for the given set of inputs. Learning algorithm modifies the weight matrix to minimize the cost of the network. Gradient descent algorithm is most commonly used for modifying the weight matrix in small steps based on the cost gradient of each weight. The cost gradient of a weight gives us an indication of the change in cost for a small change in that weight.

Back-propagation is the mechanism to efficiently compute the cost gradients of weights of all layers. The cost gradient of the weights in the output layer are computed first and then these gradients are propagated back through the hidden layers so that learning can happen across all layers.

Hyperparameters: As part of learning, we are optimizing the weight matrix to minimize the cost of the training data. However, there are several parameters called hyperparameters which help us to control the learning process. These parameters are set at the training algorithm level and are fine-tuned as part of systematic trial and error learning. Some of the hyperparameters are:

Learning Rate: Learning rate indicates the quantity of the change to be made to the weight matrix in each training step. Too large a change to the weights may miss potential minima whereas too small a change may take forever to train the network.

Regularization Parameter: Regularization techniques are used to ensure that networks generalize the results when faced with unseen data. One of the regularization techniques is to add the additional constraint of minimizing the weights, apart from minimizing the cost. Regularization parameter controls the level of influence of regularization on the training algorithm.

Batch Size: Neural network can be trained by modifying the weights and biases for each input record in the training dataset. In this approach, the weight matrix is updated based on the computed cost of each training record. Once the weights are updated, the next record is picked up for optimization. This is called 'online learning.' Online learning has 2 disadvantages:

- Re-computation of weights and biases after every iteration can be processing intensive.

- In datasets with large outliers, online learning can skew the results.

Alternatively, network weights can be updated using the average cost computed for a small batch of training records. This is called 'batch learning.' Batch learning helps to eliminate the impact of outliers as these are averaged out across several records in the batch. Batch size indicates the number of records in each batch used to train the neural network.

There are several other hyperparameters specific to different deep learning networks like CNN, RNN and LSTM, which we will discuss in respective chapters.

10.4 Gradient Descent Algorithm

Neural networks are complex mathematical functions in which we try to optimize the designed cost function by modifying the weight matrix as part of training. As we have seen earlier in the ordinary least squares algorithm, simple functions like quadratic functions have a convex shape. Such functions have only one minimum value for the cost and finding the weights corresponding to that lowest cost gives us the solution. This can be achieved by computing the derivative of cost with respect to the weight matrix and equating the same to zero. However, cost function in neural networks is not convex as it includes complex non-linear activation functions. Non-convex functions can have multiple minimum points.

Global Minima: Global minima is the minimum value for cost across the universe of possible values.

Local Minima: Cost of the network may have several local minima for different combinations of weight matrix. Near local minima, cost increases for any small change to the weight matrix even though this is not the ideal solution.

One of the key problems encountered in neural network learning is that weights are saturated near local minima without any further learning as any change to them will only increase cost. There is no way for the algorithm to find out whether a particular point for cost value is a local minima or global minima. This is exactly the reason why learning in neural networks is described as a systematic trial and error approach.

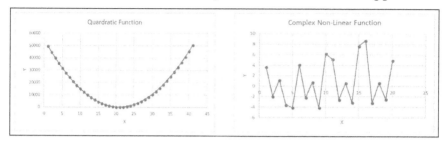

Figure 31. Global Minima vs. Multiple Minima for Neural Networks

Cost of the neural networks changes as the weight matrix changes and we may not have one minimum cost value considering complex equations. How do we compute the ideal values of the weight matrix programmatically so that the cost function can be minimized?

- Visual inspection of plotted data can be a useful way to find the nature of such a relationship between cost and weight matrix and to identify minima. This option is not practical, as this cannot be done beyond three dimensions. So, this is not a viable option.

- Brute force computation: Compute the cost for each and every combination of value of the weight matrix variables and choose the combination with the lowest cost. This option again is not practical as such computations cannot be completed within a reasonable time.

Gradient descent algorithm is one of the efficient ways to solve this optimization problem.

Training a neural network is an optimization problem. We have a dataset with training inputs and the corresponding output. The training algorithm needs to arrive at the best weights and biases in the neural network in such a way that the network can generate the outputs as close to the historical values as possible.

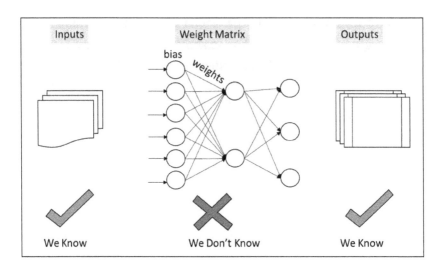

Figure 32. Learning in Neural Networks

The core purpose of the gradient descent algorithm is to minimize the cost of the neural network by optimizing the weight matrix. Cost function is a trainable representation of the error, which is the difference between computed output and actual output. Once we have the weight matrix that results in minimum cost, it also means that such a network produces minimum error for the future predictions as well.

Let us represent the cost as a function.

– Cost = function (computed output, training output): Cost signifies the difference between neural network output and given output

– Computed output = function (weight matrix, training input): Neural network output depends on given inputs and weight matrix

– By combining the above 2 dependencies

– Cost = function (weight matrix, training input, training output)

    Training inputs and outputs for a given neural network are given so we can only modify the weight matrix to minimize the cost.

Simplifying the equation further by leaving out inputs and outputs which are anyway fixed

- Cost = function (weight matrix) can also be written as below

- Cost = function (weight 1, weight 2, ...all the weights in the network)

For the purposes of neural network training, we see cost as a complex function of weights, the only variable in the equation. For the sake of simplicity and understanding, we are leaving out various types of cost functions and their actual mathematical equations but focusing on intuitive and logical representation.

Differentiation techniques in linear algebra help us to find the dependencies between the outputs of a complex function and its parameters. Differentiation of a function with respect to a parameter indicates the change in the output of the function for a small change to the parameter. Differentiation is relevant only for a small change in the value of the parameter and these computations do not hold if the parameter changes are large. Change in the output of a function for a change in the value of the parameter is also referred to as gradient of the function for that parameter.

As we have seen in the previous equation, cost is a function of the weight matrix, which includes all weights and biases in the neural network. Cost gradients for each variable in the weight matrix can be calculated using differentiation techniques applied on the cost function and activation functions used in the network. The cost gradient of a weight gives the change in the value of the cost when there is a small change in the weight. This gives us an indication as to whether the cost increases or decreases for a small increment to that weight; this is very important. Once we know the cost gradient of a weight, we can make a small change to the weight in such a way that it reduces the cost.

For example, the positive cost gradient of a weight indicates that when we increase the value of the weight, then it will increase the cost.

So, as part of the gradient descent algorithm, we will reduce the weight by a small quantity so that the cost comes down. Similarly, the negative cost gradient of a weight indicates that increasing the value of the weight decreases the cost. In such a case, we will increase the weight by a small value to bring down the cost. As mentioned earlier, change to the weight needs to be small otherwise differentiation computations do not hold and corresponding changes to the cost may be arbitrary.

As we are modifying the values of the weight matrix based on their respective cost gradients to bring down the cost of the network, it is referred to as 'gradient descent' algorithm. Once we modify all the weights and biases by a small quantity according to their cost gradient, then the cost of the network is also most likely to come down by a small quantity. Then the process of computing cost gradients and adjusting the weight matrix is repeated until we reach satisfactory cost and error values for the training data.

Each iteration of modifying the weight matrix to re-compute the outputs and corresponding cost is called 'learning step.' Each learning step has to be small for the gradient descent algorithm to work. With each learning step, the cost of the neural network is expected to come down and produce an output which is a step closer to the expected output. The neural network has to be trained over several learning steps to be able to reach the lowest possible cost value.

All weight increments and decrements done in proportion to cost gradient are scaled by a hyperparameter called 'learning rate.' Designers can use the learning rate to control the amount of change to the weight in each learning iteration. Learning rate determines the quantum of change in the weight matrix for each learning step and hence determines the speed at which learning takes place.

Gradient descent algorithm is relatively simple to understand and is quite useful in a large number of applications.

10.5 Back-Propagation

For the gradient descent algorithm to work, we need to compute cost gradients for each variable in the weight matrix for each learning step. For neural networks with a large number of variables, this can be quite cumbersome.

Here, we have 2 problems:

- Computation of cost gradient individually for each and every variable in the weight matrix is going to be cumbersome. For applications in NLP, video and image processing, the number of neurons can run into thousands or even millions. It is computationally infeasible to perform such an approach.

- We depicted a simple representation of cost function earlier in the chapter

   o Cost = function (weight1, weight 2...all weights in the neural network)

   But in practice, all weights are not at the same level in the cost function. Neural networks are nested mathematical functions with the outermost layer producing the output and the corresponding cost. Weights leading to the output layer are direct inputs, whereas weights in the previous layers go through aggregation and activation functions of their respective layers as well as following hidden layers. Computation of cost gradients for weights in hidden layers is more complex as the cost function for them is more nested than for the weights in the output later.

Back-propagation algorithm works on the concept of chain rule for differentiation in linear algebra. Gradient descent with a back-propagation algorithm is a powerful combination that can be used for learning in the neural networks.

Chain Rule for Nested Functions: Chain rule helps in finding the cost gradient of variables within a nested function. Let us say we have a nested function

- Output = f2 (f1(input))

This can also be represented as the following equations

- Output = f2 (hidden)

- hidden = f1 (input)

As per chain rule, the gradient of output function for input variable is a multiple of

- Gradient of hidden for input variable * Gradient of output for hidden function

In other words, the gradient of a function over a variable in a nested function is a multiple of the local gradients at each of those nested functions. Figure 33 depicts the chain rule for gradients.

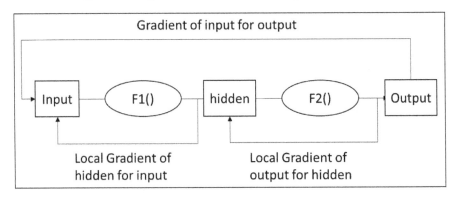

Figure 33. Chain Rule for Gradients

Neural networks are nothing but nested mathematical functions of weights variables. These mathematical functions include matrix multiplication, aggregation, activation and cost functions. Weights closer to the output are less nested than the weights that are far from the output layer.

Figure 34 gives an overview of how the inputs flow through various mathematical functions of the neural network to produce the output and corresponding cost.

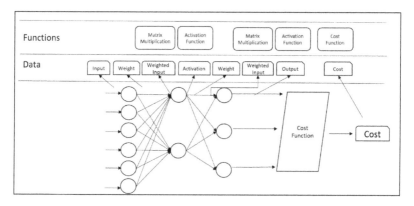

Figure 34. Data Transformation Through Neural Network Layers

Back-propagation algorithm works by computing the local gradient for each of the above transformation functions separately. Cost gradient at the output is back-propagated to each and every weight variable using the chain rule. Training data is transformed by different functions from the input layer to the output layer through hidden layers. Similarly, the gradient computed at the output layer is passed back through each hidden layer by multiplying with the local gradient at each layer using the chain rule. Figure 35 shows the computations involved in the back-propagation of the gradient.

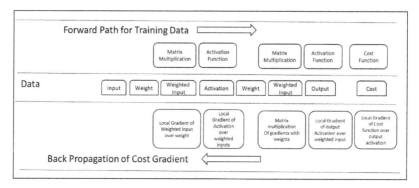

Figure 35. Back-Propagation of Cost Gradient

Detailed steps involved in the back-propagation are listed below

- As a first step, the gradient of cost function vs. output neurons are computed. This is the differentiation of cost function.

- Then the local gradient of output layer (the outputs of the output layer vs. inputs to the output layer) is computed. This is the differentiation of activation function of the output layer.

- Using the chain rule, by multiplying the above terms, we can get the gradient of cost function vs. inputs to the output layer.

- Similarly, we compute the local gradient at each hidden layer (output of each hidden layer vs. input to that hidden layer). This is the differentiation of activation function at each hidden layer.

- Gradient computed at the output layer is passed back through layers multiplying with local gradients.

Back-propagation algorithm stops at the first hidden layer as the input layer of neurons are simply capturing the data and does not have cost gradients. At this point, we have all the cost gradients to make changes to the weight matrix and prepare the network for the next learning step. As back-propagation algorithm works on computing the local gradients and processing the error back through local gradients, computationally this is as light weighted as the forward movement of the data in the neural network for predictions.

11

Neural Network Design Considerations

11.1   Neural Network Architecture

Designing a neural network is an essential step to ensure that the learning process is effective. As we have seen earlier, a fundamental aspect of the neural network is the user-defined mathematical model visually represented as a directed graph of neurons. Given the training data and problem statement, the following are the key questions for the designer of a neural network:

– Given that the input and output layers of a neural network are fixed, how many hidden layers to be included?

– How many neurons in each hidden layer?

– What is the most suitable activation function for each layer?

– What is the ideal cost function for the given problem?

– What is the ideal method to initialize the network weights and biases?

– What is the ideal way to normalize the input and output data?

These are important questions. We need to get these elements right in order to progress well with learning. The following aspects about the problem statement and training data need to be considered for the design:

– How many records in the training dataset?

– How many features in each training record?

143

- Nature of the problem (regression/two-class classification/ multi-class classification)

- Range of output values in case of regression

Number of Hidden Layers: Intuitively, more number of hidden layers indicate higher complexity and such networks can capture more complex relationships. As we introduce more layers, each layer aggregates outputs of the previous layer with an additional layer of weights and biases. Each layer of neurons represents an additional layer of aggregation and activation functions, increasing the complexity of the overall model. However, increasing the number of hidden layers has the following disadvantages in a fully connected feedforward network.

- Vanishing/Exploding Gradients: Back-propagation algorithm is used to transfer the gradient computed at the output layer to inner hidden layers. To achieve this, the cost gradient at the output layer is multiplied with the local gradient of the previous layer to arrive at the cost gradient of weights in the previous layer. This is repeated until the first hidden layer gradients are computed. We will see later in the chapter that for many of the activation functions, gradient values are less than 1. As we multiply the cost gradient at the output layer with the local gradient of each hidden layer, gradient value becomes smaller with each propagation across layers. This is usually referred to as vanishing gradients problem due to which learning in the layers closer to the input layer becomes negligible. As gradients become too small, any changes to weights and biases based on those gradients are too insignificant to make any learning possible. This is more evident in layers closer to the input layer as our learning starts at the output layer and is back-propagated. For a fully connected feedforward network, 1 or 2 hidden layers can be effective for solving many problems. Impact of additional layers need to be designed carefully and tested to ensure learning actually happens.

- Number of neurons in each hidden layer indicates the amount of freedom that we are building into the model. Increasing the number of neurons in hidden layers can have a multiplier effect on the number of variables in the weight matrix that need to be trained. For example:

Table 41. Number of Variables in Weight Matrix

Neural Network Architecture	Number of Variable in Weight Matrix
10 input neurons 5 neurons in hidden layer 1 3 output neurons	73 variables
10 input neurons 10 neurons in hidden layer 1 3 output neurons	143 variables
10 input neurons 10 neurons in hidden layer 1 5 neurons in hidden layer 2 3 output neurons	183 variables
10 input neurons 10 neurons in hidden layer 1 10 neurons in hidden layer 2 3 output neurons	254 variables

As the number of variables in the weight matrix increases, it gives more freedom to the neural network to map the data to the model. This can result in overfitting the training data to the model. As the number of variables increases, so does the complexity of the optimization algorithm. As there can be several minima, the algorithm may end up with one of the not-so-efficient minimum.

A complex network with a lot of parameters will not be a major issue if we have a large training dataset that the neural network has to fit into its training. However, when we have limited records in the training dataset, it is advisable to limit the number of variables to few.

Similarly, too simple a model with minimum parameters cannot capture the complex relationships and underfit the data. In other words, a very simple model cannot explain the training data patterns, resulting in a significant error.

Number of Neurons in the Output Layer: Number of neurons in the output layer is arrived at based on the nature of problem and label values.

– For classification problems, the number of neurons in the output layer is chosen as the number of categories in the output, with softmax as the activation function. Each neuron in the output layer maps to a category with its activation, indicating the prediction of that category.

– For regression problems with a single learning objective, the output layer has just one neuron. As the label is a continuous variable, it is preferable to have a linear activation function in the output layer.

11.2   Activation Function

Activation function is specified for each hidden layer and also the output layer. Selection of activation function needs a careful analysis of the following aspects:

Transformation: Activation function transforms its inputs using a linear or non-linear function. Non-linear activation functions are better positioned to capture the complex relationships between features and labels. However, non-linear transformation has the disadvantages of producing range bound output that too only for the weighted input values within a certain range.

Gradient: It is important for an activation to provide a good gradient so that network weights and neurons can learn. The gradient of an activation function is the change in the output of that function for a small change in the input. Non-linear activations produce a gradient only within a narrow range of input values.

Nature of the Problem: Activation function can be chosen based on the nature of the problem and also depending on the layer within the network. For example, a softmax layer is ideally suited for the output layer of classification problems whereas linear activation is preferred as the output layer for regression problems.

Let us look at different activation functions from the perspective of the above parameters.

Sigmoid Layer: Sigmoid function adds non-linearity to the network and hence is capable of capturing the non-linear relationships between the pairs of inputs and outputs. Sigmoid layer converts the input into a value between 0 and 1 in a non-linear fashion. Sigmoid takes an input range from −infinity to + infinity and produces an output between 0 and 1. The sigmoid output ranges from 0 to 0.5 when the weighted input is a negative value, and its output ranges from 0.5 to 1 when the weighted input is a positive value. We can logically consider a sigmoid neuron as triggered when its output is 0.5 or above. The sigmoid output value is exactly 0.5 when the weighted input is zero. Sigmoid function has a slope constant that controls the slope of the function. Sigmoid function is smoothest when the slope constant is 1 and hence is most commonly used.

The sigmoid output is very close to zero when the input values are −3 or below that, and similarly, the sigmoid output is very close to 1 when the input values are 3 or above that. Reducing the input value below –3 or increasing it above 3 will only result in a minor insignificant change in the sigmoid function. In other words, the gradient of a sigmoid function is close to zero when the input is not between –3 and 3.

The following table contains some weighted inputs and corresponding sigmoid outputs.

Table 42. Sigmoid Output and Gradient Values

Weighted Input	Sigmoid Output	Sigmoid Gradient
-4	0.018	0.018
-3	0.047	0.045
-2.5	0.076	0.070
-2	0.119	0.105
-1.5	0.182	0.149
-1	0.269	0.197
-0.5	0.378	0.235
0	0.500	0.250
0.5	0.622	0.235
1	0.731	0.197
1.5	0.818	0.149
2	0.881	0.105
2.5	0.924	0.070
3	0.953	0.045
4	0.982	0.018

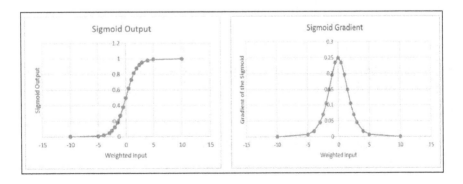

Figure 36. Sigmoid Output and Gradient for Different Values of Weighted Inputs

The amount of change in the sigmoid output is very small when the weighted input is outside the range of –3 and 3. This is a very important point to consider when designing the neural network.

Tanh Layer: Tanh is very similar to Sigmoid in functionality, but the output scaled to range from –1 to +1. Tanh mathematical function can take the values from – Infinity to + Infinity and produce an output ranging from – 1 and 1 compared to the output range of 0 to 1 for sigmoid.

Table 43. Tanh Output and Gradient Values

Weighted Input	Tanh Output	Tanh Gradient
-4	-0.999	0.001
-3	-0.995	0.010
-2.5	-0.987	0.027
-2	-0.964	0.071
-1.5	-0.905	0.181
-1	-0.762	0.420
-0.5	-0.462	0.786
0	0.000	1.000
0.5	0.462	0.786
1	0.762	0.420
1.5	0.905	0.181
2	0.964	0.071
2.5	0.987	0.027
3	0.995	0.010
4	0.999	0.001

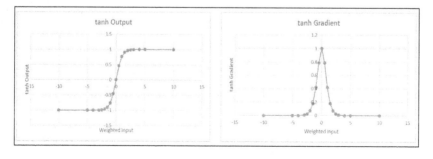

Figure 37. Tanh Output and Gradient for Different Values of Weighted Inputs

Rectified Linear Unit: ReLU produces linear output for all positive values of weighted input. ReLU outputs '0' for all negative values of weighted inputs. For all positive weighted input values, the input is passed as output directly.

Table 44. ReLU Output and Gradient Values

Weighted Input	ReLU Output	ReLU Gradient
-4	0	0
-3	0	0
-2.5	0	0
-2	0	0
-1.5	0	0
-1	0	0
-0.5	0	0
0	0	0
0.5	0.5	1
1	1	1
1.5	1.5	1
2	2	1
2.5	2.5	1
3	3	1
4	4	1

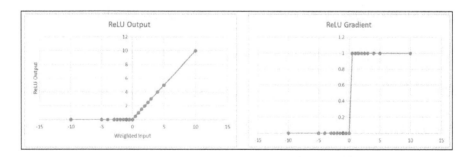

Figure 38. ReLU Output and Gradient for Different Values of Weighted Inputs

Linear Layer: Linear activation layer produces an output which is the same as the input. Linear activation is typically used in the output layer for regression type of problems.

Table 45. Linear Output and Gradient Values

Weighted Input	Linear Output	Linear Gradient
-4	-4	1
-3	-3	1
-2.5	-2.5	1
-2	-2	1
-1.5	-1.5	1
-1	-1	1
-0.5	-0.5	1
0	0	1
0.5	0.5	1
1	1	1
1.5	1.5	1
2	2	1
2.5	2.5	1
3	3	1
4	4	1

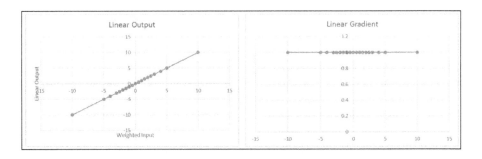

Figure 39. Linear Output and Gradient for Different Values of Weighted Inputs

Softmax Layer: Activation functions we have seen so far are based on the weighted inputs of that particular neuron. However, in the softmax layer, the activation output of a neuron not only depends on the weighted inputs of that neuron but also weighted inputs of all other neurons in that layer. Activation of a neuron in this layer is positively correlated to the weighted input of that neuron but also inversely correlated to the weighted inputs of other neurons in that layer.

Increase of a weight of a connection leading to the softmax layer will not only increase the activation of that neuron but will also reduce the activation of all other neurons proportionately. Sum of activations of all neurons in the softmax layer always totals to 1. Hence, the output of the softmax layer can be considered as a probabilistic distribution of output categories. Due to this feature, softmax is most suited as the output layer for classification problems.

There are other types of layers/activation functions:

✓ Convolutional Layer

✓ Pooling Layer

✓ RNN Layer

✓ LSTM Layer

These layers are used in deep learning algorithms, which we will discuss later in the book. As we have seen earlier, it is difficult to train a fully connected feedforward neural network with multiple hidden layers. The layers mentioned above provide an alternative to fully connected architecture to make the learning in deep neural networks possible.

11.3   Cost Function

Cost function is at the heart of machine learning training. As part of machine learning training, we bring down the cost function by modifying the weight matrix. We need to remember that cost and error are different. Error of the neural network is the difference between the expected and actual output of the network, whereas cost is a representation of that error in a manner more amenable to training and optimization. For example, in a network that is designed for the classification of handwritten digits, the error rate is the number of digits incorrectly classified by the model as a ratio of the total number of digits. However, the cost function can be root mean square (RMSE) or cross entropy.

Cost function is defined in such a way that it can be optimized in a smooth fashion in small decrements when the network weights and biases are adjusted. Cost function should be a proxy to the error in the model so that bringing it down improves the accuracy of model predictions. Cost function should be smooth, continuous and differentiable.

Activation function is specified for each layer of neurons in the neural network whereas cost function is specified only for the output. The gradient of the cost function is also an important consideration as a low gradient in the cost function can hamper the learning. Cost function takes computed output from the neural network and expected output from the training data as inputs. Cost function may also include additional parameters like regularization parameter. Regularization helps in generalizing the predictions. We will discuss it in the later sections of this chapter.

Following are most commonly used cost functions.

Root Mean Square Error (RMSE): The difference between the computed output and expected outputs of each neuron in the output layer is a good indication of the error in the network. In RMSE, these differences are squared and averaged across training records to arrive at the cost. This ensures that positive and negative differences in the results are not canceled out. RMSE is typically used in regression problems.

Cross Entropy: Logarithm is inverse to the exponential function. Exponential function raises the value of a function substantially for a small increase in the input whereas logarithmic function raises the output marginally for significant changes in the input. Cross entropy loss is computed by the multiplication of the expected output with the logarithm of actual output. This cost function is suited for classification problems with the softmax layer at the output.

11.4   Learning Mode

Learning step can be defined as an iteration in which the training data is passed through the network, the error is back-propagated and weight matrix is updated ass per computed cost gradients. In the first learning run, weights and biases are initialized randomly, but as we go through the learning steps to adjust the weights and biases, the network starts to learn about the training data. But how frequently should we update the network weights and biases? Let us say we have one million records in the training dataset. Do we pass each record through the network to compute the error and then back-propagate the error to update the weights? This can mean a significant amount of processing is required to complete the training.

Is there a better way to optimize the learning schedule? In the technology space, online and batch processing are familiar terms. In online processing, each transaction is processed separately and responded to. For example, credit card payment request at the merchant location is sent to the card scheme for approval and a response is received within seconds so that the merchant can process the customer's order delivery. Each and every customer payment request is sent to the card scheme separately for every swipe at the machine. However, interbank payment requests are collected until the payment deadline and processed in a batch after the deadline. All the payment requests are aggregated, and one payment entry is made in the ledger. Online processing is more responsive, but batch processing is more efficient. The same concept can be extended to machine learning.

Online Learning: Picking up from the above example, online learning is similar to credit card processing. Each record in the training dataset is picked up, navigated through the network to generate output and cost is computed. Gradients are computed using back-propagation and the weight matrix is modified accordingly. With this, one learning step is completed and another training record is picked up for the next learning step. Assuming that the size of the training data we have is one million records, we will have one million training steps for one parsing of the entire data. Online learning has the following disadvantages:

- Learning can be erratic depending on the nature of the training data and sequence

- Outlier training records can cause blips in the learning rhythm of the network

- Processing intensive

Batch Learning: In batch learning, we group the training records into batches for the purpose of training. Each batch of training records is passed through the network to compute the predicted output and cost gradients for all the records in the batch. Average gradient for all the training records in the batch is computed and weight matrix is updated based on these average gradients. Batch learning has the following advantages:

- Impact of outliers in training data is minimized as gradients are averaged across the batch

- Faster convergence as the training dataset is processed in fewer learning steps

11.5   Learning Pitfalls

Learning in neural networks can get derailed due to certain pitfalls. Let us look at them and how to get around them.

Overfitting: As part of education, students are encouraged to understand the concepts and not to memorize. Learning the concepts is more useful and can be broadly applied in several scenarios. Learning the concepts helps to understand and respond to problems not seen before. Alternatively, students who memorize the formulas or concepts may perform better under test conditions but fail miserably when faced with variations. This is very much true in machine learning as well.

It is possible for a machine learning algorithm to memorize the training data and produce a perfect result in that phase but then produce poor results in testing or production. A machine learning algorithm that learns the features of the data can produce better results when presented with new variations of data. This is also called the generalization capability of the model.

Why does overfitting happen?

Lot of Freedom: Overfitting can happen in a model where there is a lot of freedom, i.e. too many variables in the weight matrix or too few records in the training dataset. This means there can be many minima for the optimization algorithm which may settle for a less than optimal solution.

Too Many Learning Steps: As we have seen earlier, learning happens in steps. Each learning step reduces the cost function by a small quantity. For each learning step, weights and biases are adjusted to learn the features of the training dataset. As the learning continues, there is a point beyond which learning stops and memorizing starts. At this stage, continuing with the training will not provide any additional learning but will result in overfitting.

Cross-validation is one of the standard techniques to measure and track overfitting. For cross-validation, the training data is split into 2 parts called training and validation records. Training records can be 70–80% of the total dataset whereas validation data can be the remaining 20–30%. This is different from the test data that we use to benchmark the model or compare the results of several models in an ensemble.

The split of training records into training and validation can be randomized if it does not impact the meaning or quality of the data. As part of training, the error of the network for both training and validation data needs to be computed separately. Training should be stopped when these values are diverging, which indicates that the network is memorizing the training data.

Learning iteration consists of several learning steps to complete one parse of a given input training record. For example, given 10000 records in the training dataset, we can split the dataset as 8000 training and 2000 validation records. Among the 8000 records chosen for training, we take a batch 10 records each for every learning step. In other words, weights and balances are adjusted after computing the network error and cost for every 10 records. So, in one learning iteration of 8000 training records, the weight matrix is adjusted 800 times, resulting in that many decrements to the network cost.

During training, we need to capture 4 attributes after every iteration.

- Compute the cost of the training data (of 8000 records) using the trained model

- Compute the error of the training data (of 8000 records) using the trained model

- Compute the cost of the validation data (of 2000 records) using the trained model

- Compute the error of the validation data (of 2000 records) using the trained model

To ensure that we are not overfitting the model, we can track the below points.

- Reduction of cost of the training data should bring down the error rate appropriately. As we are optimizing the cost, if we notice that the error rate remains stagnant or increases, then it is an indication of overfitting coming into play.

- As you can see, the network has seen the training data of 8000 records, but it has not seen the validation data. So, a robust model is expected to produce the error rates of training and validation data as close as possible. As we progress through the learning iterations, if we see these 2 error rates diverging, then it is an indication of the model learning more about the training data rather than the structure

Another important technique to avoid overfitting is regularization. We will discuss regularization techniques later in this chapter.

Underfitting: Similar to overfitting, we can also have an underfitting problem. In underfitting, the neural network is not able to model the given training data. The cost and error rates are high and do not come down with learning iterations. In effect, the model results are unreliable as there is very little learning happening.

Underfitting can happen for several reasons:

- Programmatic error. Neural network related programming involves an understanding of the architecture and various design aspects. Errors can happen at any point in the flow, which can be very difficult to trace/visualize.

- Feature set is incomplete or does not represent the characteristics of the label. Features collected in the training data may not be sufficient to explain the label values. A model built on such data cannot capture any variations in the label values caused by those missing features. Feature engineering and domain knowledge are critical aspects of neural networks. In the case of underfitting, there is a need to review the features selected and also how they are presented to the network.

- Incorrect network architecture may also result in underfitting. As discussed earlier, each activation function has a range of outputs. The number of neurons in hidden and output layers have to be selected in such a way that the resultant output can cover the entire range of output values in the training dataset.

- Local Minimum vs. Global Minimum: We talked about global and local minima for cost function during optimization of the weight matrix. Neural networks can have several hundreds or thousands of variables in a weight matrix that need to be optimized to arrive at the minimum value of cost function. We cannot visualize data of more than 3 dimensions to visually inspect the minimum value. An optimization of such nature is not convex and has several minima. Based on the initialization of the weight matrix, we start randomly at a point and start moving downward from the starting point. This can lead us to a minimum, also called local minima, which can be far higher than the possible global minimum.

The following options can be tried to get over local minima:

- Re-start the learning with a different starting point (by re-initializing the weight matrix)

- Higher learning rate may cause the cost function to get over the local minima and take us a step closer to the next minimum

Vanishing Gradient: Gradient is at the heart of the learning of neural networks. The cost gradient decides the amount of change to be made to the weight matrix to reduce the cost of the network. The cost gradient is computed at the output layer and passed back to the earlier layers using the back-propagation method.

We know that the range of outputs for several activation functions are small values in the range of –1 and 1. Due to this, the cost gradient computed at the output layer is small in value. As part of back-propagation, these gradients are further multiplied with local gradients, which are also small in value, further reducing gradient values.

As the gradient moves from right to left, it gets smaller and smaller. Due to this, changes made to the weight matrix become negligible and the network is not able to learn anything. In a fully connected feedforward network with several hidden layers, learning in the layers closer to the input is going to be significantly small. Similarly, exploding gradients can also occur if we have a gradient that is higher than 1 and gets multiplied across layers. This can result in very large values for the gradients.

Gradient Clipping: Gradients vanish or explode across neural network layers and across learning iterations. A small gradient does not help us much in training. Gradient clipping is a process which is applied after computing the gradient for each weight and bias. A range of minimum and maximum is specified for the gradient and any time the gradient falls outside this range, then it is set to the boundary value. For gradients smaller than the lower threshold, it is set to the minimum and for gradients above the higher threshold, it is set to the maximum. Gradient clipping helps in a limited extent to ensure that gradients do not go out of bound temporarily, but it may not be able to solve the problem of lack of learning.

11.6 Regularization

The entire world works within a boundary of certain constraints and limitations. We all live, work and survive within the constraints set by nature, society, family and ourselves. Given all the parameters being the same, the world rewards those who work under more constraints. Training under additional constraints is an effective way to improve the performance. Many marathoners train in hilly terrains to improve speed and stamina for a marathon on a flatter terrain. Sprinters practice running in sandy beaches so that they can be much faster on the track. These are additional constraints they place upon themselves to ensure that their performance in real life can match or better their training performance.

Can we place additional constraints on our neural networks during training so that they can perform better when they face unseen situations? Regularization is precisely that. Regularization techniques can help the model generalize better, thus avoiding overfitting. As discussed earlier, training a neural network is an optimization problem. Firstly, we define a cost function that most accurately captures the difference between the computed results and historical results of the training data. Then we optimize the network weights and biases under the constraint that each change to the weight matrix also brings down the cost. We use gradient descent and back-propagation algorithms to achieve this.

We verify the network learning with validation data to ensure that this network performs equally well when a new set of data is fed. The only constraint we have for our optimization problem is that the cost function should be brought down for each change to the weight matrix. Regularization places an additional constraint on the optimization problem so that the network can better abstract the features of the training data. Depending on the type of constraint placed on the network, there are several regularization types available.

Weights Regularization: In a neural network, there are connections between the neurons in different layers and each connection has a weight. Similarly, each neuron has a bias except for those in input layers. In weights regularization, the optimization algorithm has to find the weight matrix that not only minimizes the cost function but also minimizes the weights and biases of the network. So, for every change in the weight matrix, the optimization algorithm has 2 parameters to minimize, one is the cost and the other is an aggregation of all the weights and biases in the network. We know that the first parameter cost is dependent on the second parameter.

Regularized Cost = Cost + Regularization parameter *Aggregated Weights in the network

Optimization algorithm not only has to minimize the cost by modifying the weight matrix but also minimize the second term by reducing the weights. Regularization parameter is a hyperparameter that indicates how much importance we should give to the regularization of weights. Some features have a greater influence on the label than others. Features that have a greater influence on the label have a more consistent gradient than the features with minimal influence on the label. This relative importance is also applicable to weights and biases in the network as they carry the features through the network to the output layer. In other words, some weights have more influence on the output label than others. Let us consider the following scenarios:

— Weights with greater influence on output and positive gradient: As the gradient is positive, decreasing the weight (or bias) decreases the cost. These weights are reduced as per both the terms in the above equation. Reduction in weight due to regularization is scaled by a hyperparameter called 'Regularization Parameter.'

— Weights with greater influence on output and negative gradient: As the gradient is negative, the value of weight (or bias) is increased to reduce the cost. However, weight is also reduced for regularization as captured in the second term in the above equation. Net change to the weight will be positive only if such a change is bringing the cost down significantly, compensating the decrease by regularization term.

— Weights without much influence on output and positive gradient: As these weights have zero/little influence on the cost function, the optimization algorithm will simply reduce such weights as part of learning as well as regularization terms. Due to this, these weights are converged to zero.

— Weights without much influence on output and negative gradient: As these weights have small gradients, increase in the weights by the learning term is small compared to the decrease in weights by regularization term. These weights are quickly converged to zero.

Regularization parameter is very similar to the learning rate. Learning rate is the hyperparameter to scale the cost gradients using which we increase or reduce the weights in the network. Regularization parameter is the rate at which we bring down the weights in the network after every learning iteration.

Following are the variations of weights regularization:

L1 regularization:

Regularized Cost = Cost + Regularization Parameter * Sum of
All Weights in the network

L1 regularization is done by simply adding all the weights in the network multiplied by the regularization parameter to the cost function. In this approach, the optimization algorithm reduces all the weights by equal quantity in proportion to the regularization coefficient irrespective of whether a particular weight has a large value or small value. This will reduce smaller weights to zero faster than the larger weights.

L2 Regularization:

Regularized Cost = Cost + Regularization Parameter * Sum of
Squares of All Weights in the network

As we are squaring the weights before adding them to the cost, the weights with larger values increase the cost more than the weights with smaller values. The optimization algorithm reduces the larger weights more compared to smaller weights after every training iteration. Due to this, larger weights are reduced more compared to smaller weights.

L1 + L2 Regularization:

Regularized Cost = Cost + Regularization Parameter * (Sum of
Weights + Sum of Square of Weights)

This method combines the above 2 approaches. The optimization algorithm reduces the weights, both small and large, in every learning iteration except those weights that have a significant impact on reducing the cost when their value is increased.

Neural network designers can fine-tune the values of learning rate and regularization parameter to adjust the level of constraint they want to place on the network due to weights regularization.

Dropout: Dropout is another technique used to improve the learning by placing additional constraints in terms of nodes in the network. In this approach, some nodes in the hidden layers are randomly dropped in every learning iteration. For example, in a neural network with structure 50 input neurons → 20 hidden layers →10 output layers, a dropout of the rate of 40% may be specified for the hidden layer. This means that for every training iteration, 40% of the neurons in the hidden layer are dropped and hence they do not send any output to the next layer.

In our example, 8 neurons out of 20 (40%) are randomly selected and their output is set to zero during the training round. Cost is computed from the resultant output, which was produced without the feed from those dropped neurons in the hidden layer. This cost is minimized by adjusting the weights of the remaining neurons. In the next round of training, another set of randomly selected neurons are dropped from the hidden layer and so on. This approach ensures that neurons are able to learn about the features of the system, even in a partial network. Once the network is trained, the full network is deployed to generate predictions from the new data.

11.7   Feature Engineering

Feature engineering is about selection and presentation of features to ensure smooth and efficient machine learning. As machine learning designers have access to large data from enterprise sources along with unlimited public sources of information and unstructured data, it is important to select and engineer the features carefully. There is no magic formula to arrive at the most appropriate feature list for training. There are several techniques listed below which can be experimented with to find the best the option. Following are some considerations for feature selection.

Number of Features: It is important to select the right quality and quantity of features. Knowledge of the business and domain knowledge are important to understand which features are important in explaining the output. Domain experts need to analyze the problem statement and list the potential features in the order of priority. This need not be 100% accurate but nevertheless, a list to the best of knowledge at the time.

Correlation analysis, discussed earlier in the book, also provides an indication of the level of influence each feature has on the label. As for number of features, selecting too few features can result in a solution that cannot model the given label and underfits the training data. As the model excludes some of the important features, the error in the result can be unacceptably high. We may find it difficult to train the network to have a low error for training data itself, let alone the best results for unseen data.

Similarly, too many features also pose a problem. Having a large number of features—out of which some are critical, some are moderately important and some are irrelevant—can skew the model and the results may not be satisfactory. We are starting the network with randomized weights for each of the feature, which means the network does not have any clue about the significance of each of the feature to start with.

The ideal situation for us is that the network learns the importance of each feature and assigns the weights accordingly. We are not talking about one solution here but an optimization problem which can have multiple solutions. Depending on the initialization, training data sequence and amount of training, we may end up in one of the less than acceptable minima for our cost function. A large number of features means more degrees of freedom for the optimization algorithm and more chance of it landing in such less than optimum solutions.

Number of Training Records: Large number training records is a big boon for neural networks algorithm. More training records add to the constraints that the network has to operate within. The network has to predict the right output for a very large number of training records so that it can be safely assumed to have learned the features. However, when we have limited training records, features have to be very selective. For example, given a training dataset of 5000 student records with an aim to predict the outcome of an exam, it is too much to select 500 features about each student. This results in too few student records trying to find the relation between too many features and label. In this case, training data records may not be sufficient to find the optimum solution. However, 25 feature set for a 5000 student training data is a good place to start.

Presentation of the Features: It is important to have the domain knowledge not only to choose the features that are most relevant but also to decide how best to present them. Features have to be engineered so that they have maximum correlation with the label. Fully connected feedforward neural networks treat each training record as a separate example for learning and they cannot capture any temporal relationships between them. Such dependencies across training records need to be presented as additional derived variables in each training record.

Let us assume that we are predicting the stock price based on historical fundamentals of a company like 'Revenues' and 'Net Profit.' The neural network cannot automatically predict how the rate of change of net profit is impacting the stock price. For this, we need to explicitly add an additional feature indicating net profit change over the previous quarter/year.

Some examples of feature selection and presentation are described below.

Let us look at the following example in which we have just 2 fields.

- Net Profit for the Quarter – Input Feature

- End of Day Stock Price – Output Label

In reality, stock price varies based on a number of other parameters like market volatility, company-specific events, industry-specific events and rating changes. However, for our analysis, let us assume all others are constant and see how we can engineer the features.

- Net profit is an information that is available quarterly and stock price is available is on a daily basis. Net profit is unlikely to have a strong correlation with a price that fluctuates every day. A better model can be to predict the average stock price over a quarter, depending on the net profit of the previous quarter. These attributes have a better chance of correlation compared to the original set.

- Net profit for a quarter may have a good correlation with the average price in the following quarter but that may not be sufficient. Markets reward companies that are growing their profits consistently compared to the companies with stagnant profits. So, we can consider adding 2 additional derived fields:

    o Change in profits compared to last quarter

    o Change in profits compared to the same quarter last year

    We will add these 2 features in addition to the absolute value of the net profit.

    - We may also consider adding 2 additional second level derivatives:

        o Growth/fall in quarterly profits compared to last quarter

        o Growth/fall in quarterly profits compared to the same quarter last year

    Here, we are not only capturing the change in profits but also the rate of change.

Table 46 presents the best feature–label combination for the given sample data.

Table 46. Feature Engineering Example

Features	Label
Net Profits	
Change in profits compared to last quarter	
Change in profits compared to same quarter last year	Average quarterly share price
Growth/fall in quarterly profits compared to last quarter	
Growth/fall in quarterly profits compared to same quarter last year	

Let us take another example of a model predicting the price of a property based on historical transaction. We have the following data:

Table 47. Data Structure for House Price Prediction Example

Features	Label
Transaction Date	
House Size	
No. of Bedrooms	
Year of Construction	
Post Code	
State	Price of the House
Swimming Pool (Y/N)	
Gym (Y/N)	
Distance to School	
Distance to Hospital	
Distance to Public Transportation	

As we have seen earlier, there is no single way to model any problem in machine learning. Here are some thoughts on presenting the features to the model:

- Transaction Date: Neural networks expect numerical fields as input and cannot process date fields directly. One option is to consider splitting the date into day, month and year and capture them as 3 different features. But on closer look, such features do not seem to have any direct correlation with the price of the house. In other words, assigning a weight to each of the day, month and year fields of the transaction date may not give any correlation with transaction prices. Instead, we can convert this field to indicate how old the transaction was to have better a correlation with the price. For example, this transaction was done 34 months prior to the current date.

–   Year of Construction: Similar logic can be applied to year of construction.

–   Postcode: Postcode is a categorical variable with a large universe of possible values. There is no value in feeding the postcode attribute as is to the neural network as input. Instead, we can do some pre-processing and bucket postcodes into fewer groups based on province or similarity in real-estate price trends.

12

Deep Learning Overview

Deep learning algorithms have revived the public interest in machine learning by producing spectacular results in machine vision, natural language processing and language translation. Fully connected feedforward neural networks with a lot of hidden layers come with their own challenges and do not serve the purpose of solving complex problems like machine vision and language translation well.

Let us look at the drawbacks of deep fully connected networks, i.e. fully connected feedforward neural networks with several hidden layers.

Temporal/Sequential Relationships: Fully connected feedforward neural networks look at the training dataset record by record. These networks do not capture the relationships between the data records. Capturing such relationships between different records in a sequence is essential for solving certain problems like natural language processing, machine translation and forecasting. In natural language processing, a sequence of occurrence of words is required for use cases like understanding the context, translation and recommending next possible words. A simple neural network is not designed to cater to the sequential relationships between the records in the training dataset.

Similarly, in forecasting problems like prediction of sales, stock prices or market demand, the inference also has temporal dependence on what happened in the last few days, months, quarters or whatever timeline. This requires capturing the relationship between the records to be able to predict more accurately.

Spatial Relationships: A fully connected feedforward neural network does not capture the spatial relationships between the different input data like pixels. An image can be presented to a fully connected feedforward neural network only as a series of pixels without any indication of how close each pixel is to other pixels. An image of 50×50 pixels can be presented as an array of 2500 features, each carrying the grayscale density of the pixels. However, in reality, these pixels are not linear and convey more meaning when looked at in the context of surrounding pixels. Higher grayscale for a group of pixels nearby indicates the presence of an object. Such inference cannot be derived from a simple fully connected network.

Vanishing Gradient: In a fully connected feedforward neural network, error is computed at the output layer and is transferred through the hidden layers using the back-propagation algorithm. Each hidden layer of neurons has an aggregation and activation function. The aggregation function sums up inputs, weighing them with induced trainable variables. The activation function provides non-linearity to the weighted sum of inputs.

As the error passes through local gradients of the activation function of each hidden layer, it shrinks in size. This happens as the error gradient is multiplied with a derivative of the activation function at each hidden layer, which is usually less than 1 in value. As the gradient moves from the output layer to inner layers, the gradient gets reduced in value significantly. As the gradient is near zero in the layers away from the output layer, these layers have zero or little learning. Due to this reason, it is difficult to train a deep fully connected network.

Overfitting: Number of variables in the weight matrix increases as we increase the number of layers in the neural network. In a fully connected network, connections are established between every neuron in one layer to every other neuron in the next layer. More trainable variables give more degrees of freedom to the fully connected deep network. This can result in several solutions to fit the training data and the model may zero in on the nearest point to minimize the training error. An overfit model gives perfect results for the training dataset but fails in validation and testing phases. Deep neural networks require a different way of connecting the neurons from one layer to the next layer to address this problem.

Deep learning algorithms are designed to address some of the above-mentioned problems. Deep learning algorithms solve the problem of spatial/temporal relationships, vanishing gradient and large number of parameters by using advanced network architecture and interconnections between neurons. Some of the most popular algorithms in deep learning we will discuss in detail are:

- Convolutional Neural Networks: These networks address the issue of spatial relationships and large number of parameters when processing image and video related use cases.

- Recurrent Neural Networks: These networks address the issue of temporal/sequential relationships between records. However, RNNs have the disadvantage of the vanishing gradient problem, making it less useful.

- LSTM (Long Short-Term Memory) Network: LSTMs are a variation of RNNs designed to address the problem of vanishing gradients. LSTMs present advanced network architecture that captures the temporal/sequential dependencies in long sequences without losing the gradient. LSTMs have been found to be very useful in speech recognition, language processing and language translation use cases.

We will look at these deep learning algorithms in the next few chapters.

13

Convolutional Neural Networks

13.1 Overview

Fully connected feedforward neural networks take a number of normalized data points as pairs of input and output data to arrive at optimum network weights. For example, a picture with 50×50 pixel dimension has 2500 pixel values as input features and corresponding label as output for classification. But is this the best approach for processing and classifying images and videos? We humans do not look at the images that way.

We do not look at the picture as a series of pixels to understand what is in the image. In fact, we do not even look at all the pixels to find out what is there in the image. With a quick glance at the picture, we will be able to accurately say if it is a person, group of people, face, animal or whatever. We observe key features in the image to be able to arrive at such conclusions quickly. So, why should our neural network look at the image as a series of pixels to understand the contents of the image? The approach of feeding the image data as a series of pixels also loses the important positional information between the pixels.

CNNs extract the key features in an image to understand it exactly like how humans are able to understand the image by looking at key features. These networks are also designed to capture the positional interrelationships between the pixels in an image.

Below are some of the examples of image classification problems that can be effectively addressed by Convolutional neural networks.

✓ Image has a Face or Not

✓ Image has an Animal or Not

✓ Image has a Group of People or Single Person

✓ Handwritten Character or Digit Recognition

13.2   CNN Design

Convolutional neural networks are designed with several layers of neurons, with each layer serving a specific purpose and unique way of connections between them. Convolutional neural networks can have several layers, but these are grouped as follows:

- Convolutional Layer

- Pooling Layer

- Fully Connected Layer

- Softmax Layer

Figure 40 depicts the schematic of the layers in a convolutional neural network.

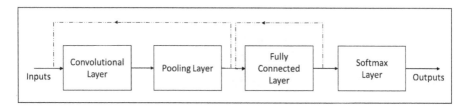

Figure 40. Convolutional Neural Network

Let us look at each layer in detail:

Convolutional Layer: Convolutional layer captures the features in the original dimension instead of as a series of inputs as in a fully connected feedforward neural network. As part of the convolutional layer, input pixel data is extracted in the form of small continuous overlapping sub-frames that are square in shape.

- Let us say our image is 100 × 100 pixels in size.

- We split the image into smaller overlapping images of 8 × 8 pixels each.

- Each such split image is separated by a gap of few pixels called 'stride.' Let us take it as 4 pixels.

- We start capturing the image snapshots in the form of 8 × 8 pixels with a gap of 4 pixels between them.

- For a 100 × 100 pixel image, this will result in 24 × 24 snapshot images (assuming that we are not padding the image with extra zeroes), each 8 × 8 pixel size, taken with a gap and overlap of 4 pixels between them.

Figure 41 represents the convolutions generated from a sample image.

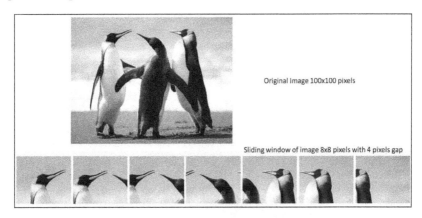

Original Image 100x100 pixels

Sliding window of image 8x8 pixels with 4 pixels gap

Figure 41. Sliding Window for Convolutions

Each of these sub-frames from the input images is mapped to a neuron in the convolutional layer using shared weights. There are that many neurons in the convolutional layer as the number of sub-frames captured from the original image. Let us look at the convolutional layer structure in our examples.

- Input image is of size 100×100 pixels.

- 24×24 neurons are in the convolutional layer mapping to each of the sub-frames.

- Each sub-frame is of size 8×8.

- There is a weight matrix of size 8×8 to map each sub-frame to a neuron in the convolutional layer.

- Pixel density of 8×8 sub-frame is multiplied with the weight matrix to arrive at the weighted sum of the neuron in the convolutional layer.

- Same weights are used to map all sub-frames to the corresponding neuron in the convolutional layer, hence they are called shared weights.

- As weights mapping each of these sub-frames to a neuron in the convolutional layer are same, it can be seen as the same filter is used to extract information from all the sub-frames.

- Each such 24×24 matrix in the convolutional layer mapping different frames from the input image using the same weight matrix is called 'feature map.'

- Convolutional layer can have several feature maps of size 24×24 neurons to capture different aspects of the image. Each feature map has its own 8×8 weight matrix of weights, which is used by all the neurons within that feature map to aggregate the sub-frames.

Each feature map represents a feature in the image. We are not specifying the exact feature to be captured by a feature map. This will be done by the learning algorithms like gradient descent and back-propagation as part of the training. Feature map represents an extraction of key features from several parts of the image using the same weight matrix. For a good image recognition solution, we need multiple feature maps to be extracted depending on the complexity of the problem. Each feature map comes with a different set of weights indicating that they capture different features. The learning algorithm trains the weight matrix associated with each and every feature map for the given input set of images.

Apart from preserving spatial relationships, another key advantage of the convolutional layer is that it significantly reduces the number of weights and biases and helps generalize the solution better. An image of size 100×100 pixels and 10 neurons in the hidden layers has 100,000 weights connecting between input and the first hidden layer in a fully connected network. However, the same image processed in a convolutional neural network with 10 feature maps of size 24×24, extracted using a filter of 8×8 matrix, has only 640 ($8 \times 8 \times 10$) weights connecting the input image to 5760 ($24 \times 24 \times 10$) neurons in the convolutional layer. This is a great reduction in the degrees of freedom and number of variables in the weight matrix despite the fact that more relevant information is collected at the convolutional layer.

Pooling Layer: Neurons in the convolutional layer can still be very large despite the extraction of features using the feature map method. In our example, we have 5760 neurons corresponding to 10 feature maps. The pooling layer aggregates the data from the convolutional layer to focus on key aspects of features instead of all the neurons in each feature map. In other words, pooling layers summarize the information from neurons in the convolutional layer. This is done by compressing every $n \times n$ non-overlapping group of neurons from the convolutional layer into a single neuron using one of the pooling methods.

Pooling layer compresses the total neurons from the convolutional layer by an order of magnitude n × n. In our example, the convolutional layer of neurons 24 × 24 for each map is compressed into 12 × 12 size for each map by using a 2 × 2 pooling area. It will result in 10 feature maps of 12 × 12 neurons. The pooling layer summarizes the information from 5760 neurons in the convolutional layer to 1440, which is 4 times less.

Figure 42 depicts the 2 × 2 pooling from the convolutional layer.

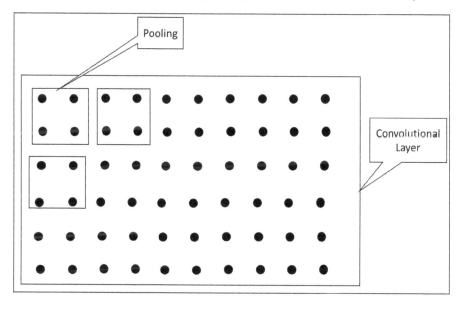

Figure 42 Pooling in Convolutional Neural Network

The idea behind pooling is to extract the dominant features from the feature maps. Pooling can be done using one of the following techniques:

Max Pooling: The neuron that has the maximum value within the n × n pooling matrix is taken as the output of pooling. In our example, the value of the neuron with the maximum value in the 2 × 2 pooling matrix is taken as the output of the pooling layer.

Average pooling: Average of the neuron values within the n × n pooling matrix is taken as the output of the pooling.

Pooling represents focusing on salient aspects of each feature map instead of focusing on each and every detail. This is very similar to how humans recognize and interpret images. Pooling considerably reduces the number of neurons from the convolutional layer. 2×2 pooling layer can reduce the number of neurons to one-fourth of the original.

We can have multiple layers of convolutional and pooling layers to transform large images or video frames into a group of feature maps of significantly reduced dimension.

Fully Connected Layer: Using convolutional and pooling layers, we have summarized the image into a few feature maps of small size. These layers have given us the extract of the image using which we can train the network for the desired result. Now we can include one or more layers of fully connected neurons to classify the image from the features extracted. In our example, instead of a fully connected feedforward network of 10,000 neurons, we now have a fully connected layer with 1440 neurons that map the extracted features. These inputs have captured the essential features of the image, ignoring irrelevant parts of the image.

Fully connected layers typically use ReLU as the activation function. The first layer of a fully connected network has that many neurons as the number of outputs from the pooling layer. These inputs are fed as a series of inputs instead of an $n \times n$ matrix like the convolutional layer. Additional fully connected layers may be added depending on the complexity of the problem.

Softmax Layer: Finally, the softmax layer produces the output. For classification problems, softmax activation is ideally suited as it provides the probability distribution for all the possible outcomes. The softmax layer has that many neurons as the number of classes into which images have to be bucketed into. As we have seen earlier, activation of neuron in this layer not only depends on the weighted input to that neuron but also inversely depends on weighted inputs to other neurons in the same layer. Outputs of all neurons in the softmax layer total to 1. As the probability of an output class increases, the probability of other classes reduces.

13.3   Training Convolutional Neural Networks

Training a convolutional neural network is very similar to training a fully connected network. It has the following steps:

✓ Randomly initialize all the weights and biases across layers of CNN

✓ For all the inputs (or mini-batch), compute the output classification

✓ Compute the cost function

✓ Compute the gradient at the output layer

✓ Back-propagate the gradient using the chain rule

✓ Make changes to the weights and biases as per the gradient

Softmax layer maps the output to one of the possible classes so that it can be compared with the expected result to arrive at the error and cost values. Similar to fully connected feedforward neural networks, the cost function is optimized by back-propagating the gradients and adjusting the weight matrix. Figure 43 presents the mathematical computations involved in the computation of output and back-propagation of the gradient.

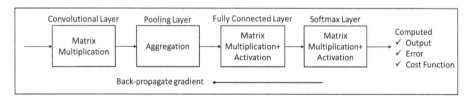

Figure 43. Mathematical Computations in a Convolutional Neural Network

CNN Example: Let us look at the MNIST dataset for designing a simple convolutional neural network. MNIST dataset consists of 60,000 handwritten digits and corresponding classification. These digits are stored in the form of 28 × 28 array, with each value indicating the gray scale of the handwritten digit. A sample architecture for a convolutional neural network can be

- 1 convolutional layer with 5 feature maps

- 1 pooling layer with max pooling

- 2 layers of fully connected neurons

- 1 softmax layer of output

We can use validation error to fine-tune the hyperparameters like the number of feature maps, number of neurons in fully connected layer and learning rate.

14

Recurrent Neural Networks

14.1 Introduction

In fully connected feedforward neural networks, the output of a neuron is dependent on the inputs given for that neuron. Information always flows from input to output in a neuron. Hence, these are also called feedforward neural networks. Such networks are able to extract the relationship between the input record and corresponding output but are inherently incapable of capturing the relationships between sequences of input records.

Temporal or sequential relationship between different input records can be recognized only when the learning algorithm is able to process them as a sequence. Recurrent neural networks attempt to address the sequence dependencies between input and output records. The idea behind RNNs is to feed every neuron not only with data from the current input record but also with the output of the neuron from the previous data records.

A simple RNN cell is presented in figure 44.

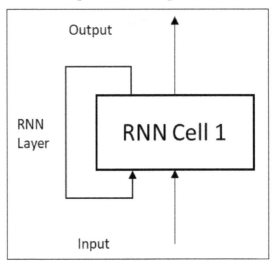

Figure 44. RNN Cell

As the input sequence is processed, data flows through the RNN cell and computed output is passed in again along with the next input record. RNN cell rolled over multiple time steps is presented in figure 45.

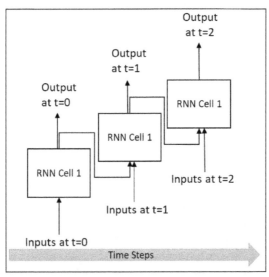

Figure 45. Single RNN Cell Rolled Over Multiple Time Steps

In the above figure, the same RNN cell is represented at different points in time. However, in the RNN network, there can be multiple RNN cells processing input records. RNN network with multiple cells rolled over is depicted in figure 46.

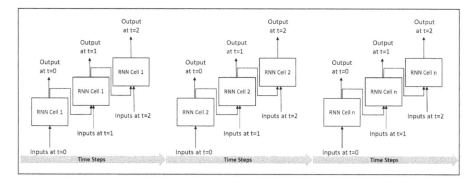

Figure 46. RNN Cells Rolled Over Multiple Time Steps

Before going deeper into how RNNs function and what the pitfalls are, let us look at different types of problems that require the extraction of sequential dependencies between inputs and outputs.

14.2   Sequence to Sequence Use Cases

As we have seen earlier, fully connected feedforward networks cannot identify sequential dependencies between the records. Broadly, there are 3 categories of sequence dependencies between inputs and outputs:

- One output at every time step

- Multiple inputs for one output

- Multiple outputs for multiple inputs

One Output at Every Time Step: In these kinds of use cases, every input record produces an output which not only depends on the current input but also the sequence of previous inputs. Output is generated at every time step based on the sequence of previous inputs. In such use cases, an error signal is generated at every time step, which is the difference between expected output and computed output. Hence, cost and gradients can be computed at each time step for training the network. One example of this use case is the recommendation of the next word based on the previous user typed words. The recommendation is generated after every word typed by the user and it is based on the past few words typed.

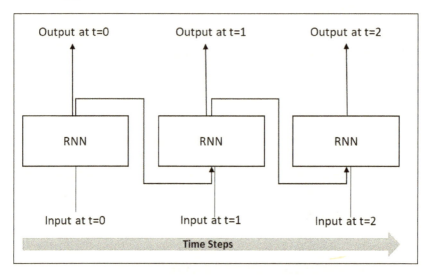

Figure 47. RNN Implementation with Output at Every Time Step

Multiple Inputs for One Output: In these kinds of use cases, the output is available only for a sequence of inputs. For example, predicting the sales for the next quarter based on the sales data for the last 3 months requires processing of multiple input records to produce the output. In these use cases, an error signal is generated only at the end of the input sequence. Hence, computation of cost, gradients and corresponding learning process happen only at the end of every input sequence.

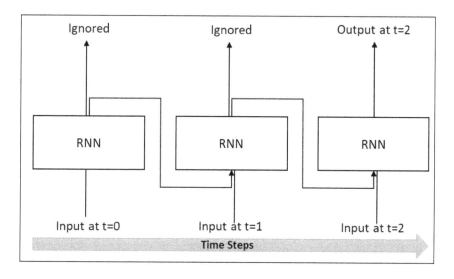

Figure 48. RNN Implementation with Output at the End of Time Series

Multiple Outputs for Multiple Inputs: For use cases like language translation, several input words in a sentence are processed and then translated words in the target language are produced. These use cases take several inputs to process them and produce several outputs. Here, an error signal is generated for all output time steps. So, cost, gradient computation and learning can happen at these time steps.

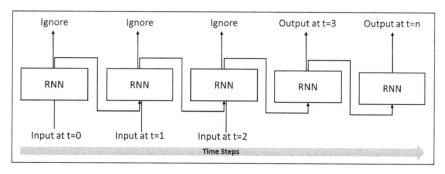

Figure 49. RNN Implementation with Series of Inputs Followed by Series of Outputs

Let us look in detail at how a basic recurrent neural network functions and the drawbacks of basic RNN.

14.3 Basic Recurrent Neural Network

Basic recurrent neural network is structured into layers of neurons as depicted below:

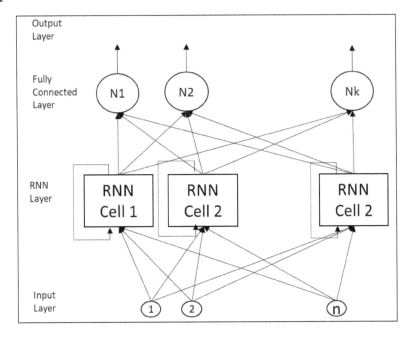

Figure 50. Basic RNN Architecture

Basic RNN consists of the following layers:

RNN Layer: This layer consists of special neurons which have feedback connections from its output to input. These neurons process not only the inputs at every time step but they also take in the output of the previous time step to compute the current output.

Output of RNN = f (previous output, current input)

RNN cells are the first layer of the recurrent neural network. All RNN cells have connections from all inputs using different trainable weights.

Fully Connected Layer: Output of the RNN cells are connected to the neurons in the fully connected layer. One or more fully connected layers of neurons processes the outputs of RNN cells. We have seen 3 variations of sequence to sequence use cases. For use cases that produce output after several time steps, all intermediate outputs produced by the network are ignored and only final output is used to compute the error and cost.

Output layer: Depending on the nature of the problem, the output layer can be a linear or softmax. For classification problems, a softmax layer is ideally suited as it gives the probability distribution across the classes. For regression problems, a linear layer without any non-linear transformation is used.

Basic RNNs have certain inherent limitations in the architecture and are unable to solve many sequence to sequence problems. Let us look at them in detail.

14.4   Limitations of Basic RNN

Basic RNNs have limitations in learning sequence dependencies, especially those that are several time steps apart, mainly due to vanishing gradient and common weights problem.

Vanishing Gradient Problem: We discussed the vanishing gradient problem in fully connected feedforward neural networks with multiple hidden layers. In such a setup, the gradient is back-propagated through network layers by multiplying with the local gradient for each activation function. Gradient value becomes small as it is propagated through several layers of neurons. As the learning is proportional to the gradient, it is minimal/negligible in the layers far from the output layer. In basic RNN, we have a similar but even bigger challenge. Here, the cost gradient has to navigate through time steps apart from the layers of neuron. For each time step, the error goes through the local gradient of the activation function and shrinks. This makes it impossible to learn the dependencies between outputs and corresponding inputs with long time gaps.

Figure 51 captures the vanishing gradient problem in RNNs.

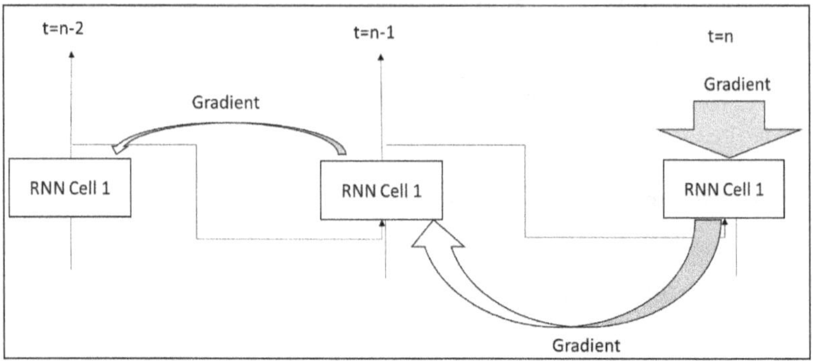

Figure 51. Vanishing Gradient – Back-Propagation Through Time

Let us suppose an input at t_{n-5} is influencing the output at t_n. To capture this relationship, the computed cost at t_n has to back-propagate through 5 time steps, each time crossing the local gradient of RNN cell activation function. This leaves very little gradient at t=n-5 for any learning to happen. This makes basic RNN ineffective in capturing long-term sequence dependencies.

Common Weights: For machines to learn sequence to sequence dependencies, the key capability is to memorize important dependencies and ignore the irrelevant ones. Let us understand this with an example. Let us say change in the interest rate cycle (from falling interest rates to rising interest rates) has an effect of slowing the economy 6 months down the line after this event. Assuming we have historical monthly macroeconomic data, we have several past instances of a pattern of reversing interest rate cycle at time step 1, having an impact on GDP growth at time step 7.

As part of learning, the system has to remember the occurrence of interest rate change at time step 1, forget all that happens with interest rates in remaining steps and associate the same with the output of falling GDP growth at time step 7. This needs a combination of memory and also the ability to forget to understand long-term sequence dependencies. In basic RNN, we have one set of weights across different time steps.

Changes to the weights to forget the near-term dependencies will also erase the memory of long-term dependencies.

LSTM is an advanced recurrent neural network that addresses these problems of basic RNN. LSTM is found to be very effective in discovering long-term dependencies and is extensively used in natural language processing and forecasting.

15

Long Short-Term Memory (LSTM)

15.1 Overview

Long short-term memory networks are advanced versions of recurrent neural networks. As we have seen earlier, in basic RNNs, the output of a neuron is fed as an additional input to the same neuron in the next time step. In other words, inputs to a neuron at a particular time t include the output of that neuron at the time t-1.

Learning in a neural network can be explained as the network's ability to transmit the cost gradient in small quantities from the output to all the layers of the network. A neural network design can be considered as good if the cost is reduced in small quantities and the weight matrix of all the layers are updated to bring down the cost. We know from earlier discussions that propagating the error several times through non-linear activation functions makes the gradient vanish. This happens due to the fact that the derivative of the activation functions like sigmoid or tanh has a narrow band.

Recurrent neural networks need to propagate the cost back in time steps, apart from sending the cost back along the hidden layers. To propagate the error back through time requires finding the gradient over consecutive time periods. This results in the loss of gradient as we move to earlier time steps in the sequence. Due to this, learning is limited to the most recent records and such networks cannot learn insights from long sequences of data.

We also have seen that basic RNN suffer from simplicity. There is only one set of weights to cater to memorizing dependencies and forgetting not so important dependencies, resulting in poor quality of learning. Long short-term memory is an advanced technique of recurrent neural networks which can learn patterns over long sequences without getting limited by the vanishing gradient problem.

15.2   LSTM Cell

LSTM algorithm is based on a new type of cell called LSTM cell. Similar to basic RNNs, the output of the LSTM cell at time t-1 is fed back to the LSTM cell at time step t along with fresh inputs at time step t. Let us see some key differences between RNN cell and LSTM cell.

– RNN cells have a single set of weights, aggregation and activation function. So, we can look at RNN cell as a single neuron. LSTM cell is not a single neuron but a collection of neurons. LSTM has 3 neurons, also called as gates (forget gate, input gate and output gate).

– Basic RNN cell produces only output at each time step. LSTM cell produces output and state at each time step. The output is used for prediction/inference of the network at that time step whereas the state represents the memory to carry the information required to produce future outputs.

– RNN cell receives input data at time t along with RNN output at time t-1 to produce output at t. Each of the 3 gates in LSTM receives input data at time step t, apart from the state at t-1. LSTM cell passes the 'Memory State' at t-1 and not the 'Output' at time step t-1, back as input at time step t.

Figure 52 depicts a single LSTM cell rolled over multiple time steps.

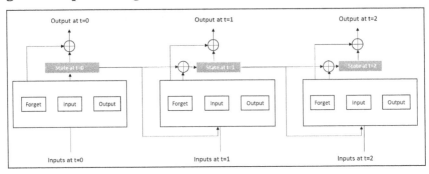

Figure 52. LSTM – Gated Approach to Recurrent Neural Networks

LSTM cell has the following 3 neurons, each acting as a gate (forget, input and output) and a memory cell called 'state.' The state stores information within the LSTM cell across time steps. Each of the gates receives the input at time step t, along with memory state at time t-1.

Forget gate: This gate controls how much information from the memory state at t-1 should be discarded at the current time step. It is a sigmoid neuron with its own trainable weight matrix.

Input Gate: Input gate is a sigmoid neuron with its own trainable weight matrix. Input gate controls the amount of information from the current training record goes into the memory in the form of a state. This is used to control irrelevant information getting stored in the memory, thus preserving the long-term dependencies in the state.

Output Gate: Output gate is a sigmoid neuron. It controls how much of the memory in the state should be used to produce output at the current time step. This is used to control when to tap memory to produce the output as per long-term dependencies.

As part of training LSTM, weights of these gates are trained to ensure that irrelevant information is forgotten, and the right information is stored in the memory to be retrieved for inference at the right time.

15.3 Constant Error Back-Propagation

Unlike basic RNN, which has one set of weights, LSTM contains different neurons and corresponding weights to forget, memorize and output long-term dependencies. With different gates controlling the learning of long-term dependencies, LSTM produces much better learning performance.

LSTM also addresses the problem of vanishing gradients in basic RNNs using constant error back-propagation through memory state. In basic RNN cell, cost is back-propagated through the cell for every time step which involves gradient reduction as it passes through the local gradient of the corresponding activation function. In LSTM cell, output is computed based on the memory state at that time and the activation of the output gate. LSTM learning algorithm propagates the cost at the output only through memory state and not through the LSTM cell.

The state is a linear aggregation of LSTM cell contributions to memory at different time points. At every time step, the state is scaled down by the activations of the forget gate and increased by activations of the input gate. This can be seen as the state forgetting some information and remembering additional information at every time step.

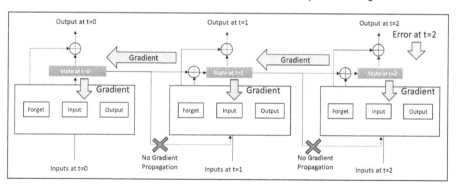

Figure 53. Constant Error Back-Propagation Through State

In LSTM, back-propagation is strictly done through memory state even though memory state at time t is based on activations of different gates which take the previous state at t-1 as input. Back-propagation algorithm propagates the cost to different time steps using the contributions to the state at that time step. This will help propagate the cost back in time through memory state without the gradient getting vanished. As memory state is linearly aggregated and does not use any non-linear activation function, the vanishing gradient problem is avoided in LSTM. Gradient back-propagation in time through the gates is ignored as it results in vanishing gradient due to non-linear activation.

With the above architecture, LSTM is able to address the twin problems of simplicity and vanishing gradients of basic RNN. LSTM is superior to RNN as

- In RNNs, the same weights control the information to be memorized, forgotten and produce a prediction. In LSTM, separate neurons called gates, with separate weights, control these functions.

- In RNNs, cost gradient is back-propagated through RNN cell for each time step and hence flows through non-linear activation function, thus vanishing the gradient in a few time steps. In LSTM, error flows through memory state and not through LSTM cell and its gates, so it's very effective in propagating across long time lags and learning the sequence dependencies.

16

Machine Learning Software Options

16.1 Introduction

Developing applications in machine learning is a lot easier now than ever. There are hosts of open source platforms, information and examples available, so it is very easy to pick up the technology and be productive quickly. The complexity lies in understanding the business problem, analyzing available data, pre-processing, feature engineering and finally developing and deploying machine learning models.

Development and deployment of models are more of design and much less of coding compared to traditional applications. Few hundred lines of code can help you build a sentiment analysis or a classification engine. Availability of open source software also makes it easy and effectively zero cost to try and experiment with these technologies. Let us look at the some of the possible options for the development and implementation of machine learning models.

Table 48. Machine Learning Programming Options

Approach	Description	Examples
Custom Programming	Custom programming from scratch for basic experiments in machine learning	MATLAB, Python, R, Matplotlib
Machine Learning Libraries	Pre-built advanced machine learning algorithm libraries to speed up research and commercial deployment	TensorFlow, Theano, Scikit-learn, MXNet, Caffe,

Approach	Description	Examples
Cloud-based Machine Learning	Cloud-based solutions with a visual editor for capturing the data and algorithms. Provides pre-built APIs for easy integration	Azure Machine Learning Studio, AWS machine learning
Ready-built Platforms	Pre-built with domain knowledge; Can be deployed on premise or cloud	IBM Watson, Cloud APIs

Let us look at these options in detail below.

16.2   Custom Programming

As discussed in various algorithms and models, the core processing of machine learning is about statistics, mathematical formulas, matrix operations and linear algebra. These functions can be developed ground up using programming languages like R, Python and MATLAB which support matrix operations and linear algebra. However, in the current situation, it is not warranted as

- There is absolutely no necessity to reinvent the wheel when pre-built open source libraries are available.

- Underlying algorithms are very complex to implement and developing them ground up is error prone.

- Requires in-depth knowledge of algorithms and various parameters.

This option is suitable for machine learning researchers who want to modify the standard algorithms to achieve specific objectives.

16.3   Machine Learning Libraries

As mentioned above, several open source machine learning libraries are available for machine learning developers. These libraries can be accessed and invoked from open source programming environments like Python. These machine learning libraries and algorithms are tested by a large community of developers and tuned over a period of time. Developers need to prepare the data, select hyperparameters to invoke the algorithm and train the model. These libraries provide features for storing the trained models and also use them for prediction in live environments.

Some of the examples are:

Scikit-learn: Scikit-learn is a popular open source library for statistical machine learning techniques. It provides algorithms for several statistical machine learning models like decision trees, Bayesian and support vector machines. This library is relatively easy to use and can be invoked from programming languages like Python.

TensorFlow: TensorFlow is the machine learning library released by Google. It is continuously improving since the original beta release. TensorFlow provides a library of neural networks and deep learning algorithms. TensorFlow works based on the concept of a computational graph, where the edges of the graph represent data (also called tensors) and nodes represent computations on data. Figure 54 depicts a typical computation graph of the TensorFlow.

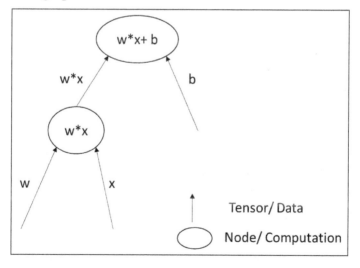

Figure 54. Computational Graph of TensorFlow

As we have seen in earlier chapters, learning in neural networks is based on the computation of gradient for cost function for each weight vector. This is complex considering the nested mathematical functions across layers of neurons. However, TensorFlow automatically computes the gradients for a given computational graph. This greatly simplifies the effort required to program the neural network and deep learning algorithms. The programmer needs to build the graph and identify the cost function to be optimized and the system automatically computes the gradients for all variables in the computational graph.

Some important terms in TensorFlow:

Variables: Variables are the trainable parameters in the model. Weight matrix of any neural network or deep learning model is defined as variables. Variables are initialized at the beginning of the training and modified as per the gradients computed by the optimization algorithm.

Placeholders: Placeholders are to feed inputs and optionally outputs of the model to the neural network and deep learning algorithms. These are defined initially at the time of graph creation, but the actual values are sent at the time of graph execution.

Session: A computational graph is executed within a session. At the beginning of the session, all variables are initialized. Then inputs and expected outputs are passed on to the computation graph either in online or batch mode. A computational graph typically consists of an input layer, several hidden layers, output layer and cost function. Optimization algorithm on cost function automatically computes the gradient for all trainable variables in the computational graph and modifies them accordingly. Each invocation of the optimization algorithm executes one learning step. For training over a number of mini-batches and epochs, the optimization algorithm needs to be invoked iteratively.

A session can be saved along with the model design captured in the form of a computational graph and all the trained weights variables. The stored model can be retrieved for further training or deployment in production for future predictions.

Deep Learning Libraries: TensorFlow supports pre-built libraries for convolutional neural networks, RNN and LSTM with several built-in parameters.

TensorFlow supports interfaces with several programming languages including Python, C++ and Java. It is relatively easy for programmers to develop applications on top of it.

16.4 Cloud-Based Machine Learning Tools

There are several cloud-based visual machine learning tools offered by cloud providers like Microsoft and Amazon. In the cloud-based solutions, various machine learning tools are offered in intuitive graphical user interfaces. These tools are visual and can be used with very little training. Programmers can develop solutions without worrying about the underlying technology and algorithm complexity. These solutions require data to be available in the cloud for training the machine learning models. Typically, cloud-based solutions have a free version for experimentation but need a subscription to cater to the production solutions.

Let us look at Microsoft Azure ML Studio and its key components:

Data Sources: Data sources form the key for any machine learning model. Azure ML studio allows for sourcing data from various sources and loading data into ML Studio to pre-process and train the models.

Machine Learning Models: ML Studio supports several machine learning models including statistical learning as well as neural networks-based models. There are several pre-built examples across industries for easy reference as well as to use them as a starting point for any new experiment.

Each model comes with a number of relevant configuration parameters, which can be set by the designer. Azure ML studio also supports automatic selection of hyperparameters from a given range of values based on the model results.

Data Analysis and Processing Tools: ML Studio has a number of analysis and processing tools to prepare the data for training. These tools are quite intuitive and can be used by simple drag and drop without a single line of code. Complex data analysis and processing can be done by dragging a few boxes and connecting them in a sequence. Some sample features are:

- Analyze and Summarize Data

- Data Filtering

- Data Transformation (Normalization, Binning, Mathematical Operations)

- Merge, Split Datasets

Deployment as APIs: Trained models can be deployed as APIs for consumption. Once the model is trained successfully, necessary components of the model can be saved and the API access for those models can be set up. Such APIs can be inference only or inference and retaining depending on the requirements and use case.

Azure Machine Learning Studio provides comprehensive tools for data sourcing, data analysis, transformation, model selection, training and deploying machine learning models.

16.5   Machine Learning Solutions/APIs

As we know, one of the important aspects of machine learning is about gathering large quantities of domain data and training the models. Platforms like IBM Watson have built-in comprehensive solutions and APIs for various use cases like natural language processing, image processing and speech recognition.

IBM Watson also comes with domain-specific solutions like healthcare. These solutions offer pre-configured models as APIs which can be used as is. In certain instances, these trained models can be further trained by proprietary data like images or text for customizing the models. Microsoft Azure, Google Cloud and AWS also offer several pre-trained machine learning algorithms for natural language processing, speech recognition and image processing.

17

Real-Life Applications and Use Cases

17.1 Introduction

Machine learning and deep learning technologies are already impacting humans in many ways for the last few years. Consumer technology firms have outpaced the academic research to develop practical applications used by people across the globe. However, the potential of the technology is huge, and we are yet to scratch the surface. These technologies can transform the functioning of governments, institutions and industries to optimize costs and improve decision making. We will see an increased adaptation of these technologies in the near future as significant investments are being made by various players.

As we have seen in the overview chapter, we can broadly categorize the use cases into 2 types:

– Cognitive Use cases

– Decision Support Use cases

Let us look at the key benefits and examples of use cases.

Table 49. Machine Learning Use Cases

Use Cases	Benefits

Cognitive Use Cases
  – Chatbot
  – Voice assistants
  – E-mail automation
  – Search
  – Computer vision (healthcare, self-driving cars)
	– 24 × 7 coverage
	  – Reduced workforce
	  – Customer experience
	  – New service models

Decision Support
  – Credit decision
  – Fraud detection
  – Forecasting
  – Risk modeling
  – Medical diagnostics
	– Improved decisions
	  – Improved operations
	  – Improved risk management
	  – New business models

Cognitive use cases in the enterprise world provide new service capability by automating part of unstructured communication with customers/partners. As cognitive systems have the capability to understand and interact in natural languages, they can chat, mail or phone just like a customer service executive. Cognitive use cases also cover computer vision and speech, helping different industries to automate the manual intensive processing to scan and tag images/videos.

Decision support use cases deal with structured data and generating deep insights for businesses to act on. Decision support use cases include detection of patterns, forecasting and prediction. In certain cases, cognitive and decision support use cases are combined to generate additional insights. For example, satellite image processing of supermarket car parking areas can give an indication of the number of footfalls. This information may be combined with several other parameters to predict the revenues of such supermarkets.

Similarly, satellite images can be processed to estimate the amount sowing in an agriculture season and predict the output. This can be combined with other parameters like demand and exports to arrive at price prediction to help decisions on hedging. Cognitive use cases can provide additional features from unstructured data, which can be combined with structured data to generate predictions for faster and accurate decisions by businesses.

Let us look at some of the popular use cases of machine learning in detail.

17.2   Sentiment Analysis

Analysis of sentiment of a tweet, movie review, product review or a book is a very popular use case for machine learning. Humans can read a tweet or a review and can immediately understand whether it is neutral, positive or negative. However, traditional systems can only understand the meaning of structured information like star rating. We may not have structured star rating in all cases. A customer's post on twitter about a company or one of its products may not have a structured star rating. Sentiment analysis systems use machine learning techniques to categorize the customer's messages based on the sentiment. This will avoid manual review of each and every tweet and review by customer service team to understand the overall feedback.

Sentiment analysis engines are built under the assumption that messages with similar sentiment contain similar words. Messages with positive sentiment usually contain adjectives like 'great,' 'excellent' or 'super.' Similarly, messages with negative sentiment contain adjectives like 'worst,' 'bad' or 'dumb.'

To build a sentiment analysis engine, we will need the following datasets:

- Historical tweets/messages which are positive in sentiment

- Historical tweets/messages which are negative in sentiment

- Historical tweets/messages which are neutral in sentiment

As we expect the historical dataset for each category of sentiment, this requires the manual tagging of training data of tweets/review into one of those buckets.

Model Dictionary: The first step in building a sentiment analysis tool is to create a model dictionary. A model dictionary is nothing but a complete list of all the unique words across datasets along with the count of occurrence for each word. A sample dictionary of words arranged in the descending order of their occurrences in the training datasets is depicted in table 50.

Please note that this is a combined list from all the datasets across sentiment categories. We may restrict the dictionary to a subset of top occurring words, like top 100 or 500 words, to be part of the dictionary. We may also restrict the dictionary to certain parts of speech like adjectives and verbs if we feel sentiment is arrived at mostly by those parts of speech. These are all decision decisions to be taken based on the problem and data samples available. Natural Language Toolkit (NLTK) is one of the most popular libraries to pre-process the natural language text and extract the information we need. In this dictionary, each word is represented by a unique number.

Table 50. Model Dictionary

Word	Number of Occurrences
See	255
Given	223
Average	145
Above	120
Good	90
All	80
Poor	75

The next step is to build the training data based on the model dictionary. We use bag-of-words representation for each message/tweet/review with the model dictionary as the baseline. Training data for each text/message/tweet consists of the number of occurrences of the words in the model dictionary along with the manually labeled sentiment.

Table 51 depicts the representation of the randomized training data for the sentiment analysis. It is important to note that even though the original input for sentiment analysis is unstructured text, we are converting it into a structured format for training the machine learning algorithm. Each training data record is of the same length as that of the number of words in the dictionary, with each value representing the count of occurrences of that word.

Table 51. Sample Training Data for Sentiment Analysis – Bag-of-Words Representation

Tweet/ Review	Number of Occurrence for the word in dictionary (Features)								Sentiment (Labels)
	See	Given	Average	Above	Good	All	Poor	...	
Record 1	2	1	0	1	2	1	0	...	Positive
Record 2	0	1	1	0	0	0	1	...	Negative
Record 3	1	0	2	0	0	1	0	...	Neutral
Record 4	...	...	...	...	...	...	...	...	Negative
Record 5	...	...	...	...	...	...	...	...	Positive
Record N	...	...	...	...	...	...	...	...	Neutral

Considering 'D' number of items in the dictionary and 'N' number of tweets/reviews for training, we have

- N training records representing each tweet/review

- Each training record has D number of features, each representing the count of that particular dictionary word in the given training record

- Each training record also has the manually tagged sentiment as the label (positive/negative/neutral)

Naive Bayes is the most preferred algorithm for text classification problems as it is simple and scalable. As we have seen earlier, this algorithm works based on the conditional probabilities. Once we have the trained model ready, we can use it to understand the sentiment of any new tweet/review. We can post the new tweet/message in a similar format as depicted below.

Table 52. Sample Record for Sentiment Prediction

Tweet/ Review	Number of Occurrence for the work (Features)							
	See	Given	Average	Above	Good	All	Poor	...
New Records	2	1	1	1	2	0	0	...

Figure 55 depicts the logical steps involved in building a sentiment analysis engine.

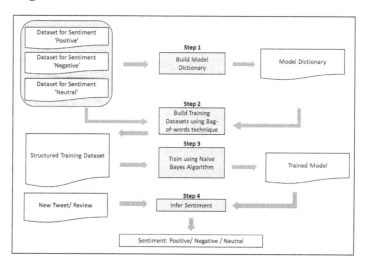

Figure 55 Sentiment Analysis Engine

17.3 Chatbot

Human-computer interaction has always been in a structured format as dictated by the computer. Interaction with computers can be in different methods like predefined commands, menus, forms and buttons. For every application, the user interface is designed based on the key user actions allowed on the application. Chatbots flip the game and make computers interact with humans in their own natural language. Chat has become an important part of human-human communication and has overtaken e-mail and SMS as the preferred mode of communication. Chatbots intend to extend the popular chat channel to include human to computer interaction. Additionally, voice bots enable users to talk to the machine and receive responses, making the interaction much more human-like.

In the context of enterprises, they need to have a communication channel open to customers for providing information, assisting them with their queries, supporting them in their sales process and so on. Chatbots are emerging to be one of the most cost-effective channels to enable such communication. Some examples of enterprise chatbots:

– Generic Query: Customer agnostic information requests like Frequently Asked Questions (FAQ)

– Generic information search and view using natural language interface

– Account Details: Query customer specific account and transaction details

– Transactions: Execute customer transactions including payments

There are several tools and packages available to build chatbots. Major technology players like Microsoft, Oracle, IBM and Facebook have created toolsets and frameworks to simplify the development and deployment of chatbots. A typical logical architecture of a chatbot looks as depicted in figure 56. Let us look at the components.

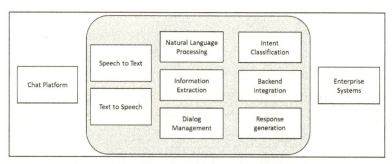

Figure 56. Chatbot Components

Chat Platform: Users access the chat application through chat platform. The chat platform can be a popular messaging platform like Facebook Messenger or consumer devices like Alexa. Chat can also be hosted as a mobile app or accessed through the company home page.

Speech to Text: This component converts user speech to text format. This is an optional component required for voice-enabled chatbots.

Text to Speech: This component converts the responses generated by the chatbot application into voice messages back to the user.

Natural Language Processing: This component extracts the natural language text message into sentences and segregates parts of speech, named entities, as required. This component is mainly used to convert the unstructured input to a structured vector of words.

Information Extraction: User interaction with a chatbot may require passing on certain information like date, amount and name. This information is necessary to serve the requests of the customers through the chatbot. Generic queries like FAQs may not have any parameters to be passed on whereas customer specific queries or transactions need additional information to complete the transactions. This component extracts the parameters to be passed on for processing.

Dialog Management: Customer may not pass on all the information required to complete the transaction in one go. For example, to book a taxi using a chatbot, the user needs to pass on booking date, time and location. In a structured interaction, the user interface mandates to capture all these fields before submitting the request. However, in a conversational style interaction, the user need not give all the details in one go. Dialog management interacts with the user to fetch the missing details in an interactive manner.

Intent Classification: This is the crux of the chatbot. Typically, a chatbot is built to serve a set of predefined purposes, also called as intents. A banking chat may have intents like balance query, last 5 transactions and funds transfer. A chatbot can only process user requests corresponding to one of the intents it is designed for. Asking a banking bot for weather information does not give a meaningful response, as that intent may not have been considered a part of the scope. Intent classification can be built using one of the machine learning algorithms like naive Bayes algorithm or deep neural networks.

Backend Integration: Customer queries or transactions using a chatbot requires information to be retrieved/passed onto backend application. Customer request for account balance needs to be retrieved from the core banking application. Customer request to book a taxi requires invocation of the corresponding service. These can be served using the same services that enable traditional customer-facing applications.

Chatbots need to be designed to cater to customer experience and demographics. Not all transactions/intents are suitable for chatbots without degradation of user experience.

17.4   Recommender Systems

Recommender systems help in recommending the most relevant product or contents to the users. Recommender systems can be quite useful in many contexts like e-commerce, music, movies, books or mobile apps. In these cases, there are thousands or millions of products and hence it is not possible for customers to browse each and every product available in the catalog. Predicting the customer interest in a product and recommending the same can be an effective way of using customer attention while they are using the application.

Personalized recommendations tailored to each customer are more effective than general-purpose recommendations. Many organizations have realized the importance of recommendations and have gained a large part of their sales from the recommendations made to the users. There are several techniques to build a recommendation engine. Following factors are considered as probable inputs to the recommendation engine:

- Customer demographics (age, location, gender, etc.)

- Product characteristics (genre, author/director, cast, etc.)

- Customer likes/dislikes for each product in the catalog based on the history of their actions

- Product-wise view of likes/dislikes by each customer based on the history of their actions

Customer likes/dislikes can be collected using combination of different techniques like:

- Customer purchase is considered as positive

- Customer feedback is considered as positive/negative based on the rating

With this, we have a large feature dataset that captures all customer ratings for each and every product. This dataset is sparse as only a small number of customers have rated a small number of products. We can use the machine learning model to predict the top few products that have the highest possibility of being rated high by a given user. Figure 57 gives the logical architecture of a recommendation system.

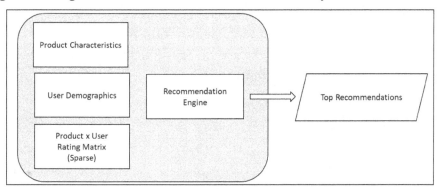

Figure 57. Recommendation Engine

A recommendation engine is trained based on the product characteristics, user demographics and available data on product x user rating matrix. Based on the trained model, it predicts the best possible product recommendations for a customer.

One of the best examples for recommendation engine is published by Google Engineers and is used for recommending apps in Google Play Store. They have open sourced the technique called 'Wide and Deep Neural Networks,' which has been implemented to recommend from millions of apps in the Play Store to billions of users.

A good measure of the effectiveness of a recommender system is the interest shown by the customer on the recommended products. This can be in the form of clicking on the products or purchasing them. Organizations need to measure and attribute the positive impact due to recommendation engines and tune the algorithm accordingly.

17.5   Image Classification

Image Processing: We have seen in earlier examples that text requires a significant amount of pre-processing in terms of extracting sentences and words, representation of words in the form of numbers and so on. Unlike text, images do not require much pre-processing. With the advent of deep learning algorithms, there is no need for manual extraction of features from the image. Individual pixels and their pixel density are presented as input to the network for training and inference. Convolutional neural networks are the most suited machine learning technique for image recognition. Convolutional neural networks provide the following advantages:

- Images are two-dimensional in nature and hence the relative position of pixels is also very important apart from the absolute values of the pixels. CNN algorithm can capture the relative position information of the pixels by processing the image as two-dimensional data. Simple feedforward networks only process the data linearly.

- CNNs simulate the way humans perceive images. Humans do not look at each pixel and its density to arrive at the contents of the image. Human vision abstracts key details of the image and then focuses on a few important areas of the image for a quick glance. CNNs works in a similar fashion and they have layered architecture. The initial layer of CNN extracts the important features from the image first and then looks at each feature a bit more to extract the next level of abstraction. The final layer of CNN is a classifier to bucket the image into one of the possible categories.

For the classification of images into one of the given categories, we need to train the network with a given set of training data. Training data consists of a large number of images and the corresponding tag classifying the image to one of the possible output classes. Post the training, the model is able to categorize each image into one or more bucket as per the training schedule.

For example, an image recognition model could be trained with 100,000 images with each one classified as 'Face' or 'Not Face.' A well-designed convolutional neural network extracts the key features from the image to classify each of them accordingly.

In the current scenario, it is not needed to train an image recognition application from scratch. There are a number of pre-trained APIs available for this task. It is also possible to start with a trained model as the basis and further train with use case specific images. Open CV is one of the popular open source libraries for computer vision and image recognition. It comes with a number of pre-trained image recognition libraries.

Video Processing: Video is a continuous stream of images rolled with a certain speed of frames per second. Video processing and recognition use case can be seen as an extension of image recognition use case. Open source tools like FFmpeg support breaking down the video image into its elementary frames. Post that, these frames can be processed as individual images and contents can be predicted using image recognition algorithms. One of the popular use cases for video processing is face recognition from a CCTV camera installed in a bank or an airport. The video stream from the CCTV can be sliced into images and these images can be used for identification of the face.

Figure 58 depicts the typical architecture of an image classification use case.

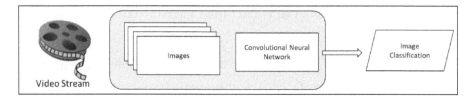

Figure 58. Image/Video Classification

17.6   Forecasting of Financial Markets

Forecasting of financial markets is one of the potential use cases of machine learning algorithms. It is not possible to predict exactly how financial markets behave at every point in time. However, historical trends can give signals with a certain level of confidence level which can perform better than a random guess. There are many ways to structure the problem statement and we will take one example to illustrate the forecasting. Let us say we are building the model for predicting the stock index change over a specific period (1-month) in the future. We define the following buckets for change in the index value over that period.

- Bucket 1 – Falls by more than 10%

- Bucket 2 – Falls between 0 and 10%

- Bucket 3 – Gains between 0 and 10%

- Bucket 4 – Gains more than 10%

We have a classification problem in which we have to classify 1-month future change in the index into one of the above 4 buckets based on the feature data available today.

We can collect daily historical data of several features of the index like index Price/Earnings Ratio (P/E), index past returns for different time periods, macro indicators like interest rates, inflation and other similar parameters that could influence index value. Based on the historical price data, we can also retrospectively compute the buckets for 1-month future returns for these historical records.

A typical classification model using neural networks processes each training record separately. However, in forecasting scenarios, the sequence of records also could play a role apart from the contents of the records. LSTM is best suited for learning the long-term dependencies between the records and providing the forecast. Once the model is trained, we can pass on the feature set as of today and get the prediction of the bucket for the stock index as of 1 month in the future. This may not be taken as absolute investment advice but can be very useful in augmenting other techniques of evaluation performed by the investor/analyst. Figure 59 depicts the architecture for the stock index prediction model.

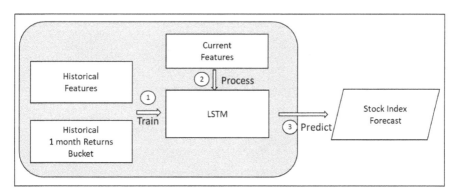

Figure 59. Forecasting Stock Index

Research and investments in machine learning by various industries, technology giants, startups, governments and universities are significantly on the rise in recent years. This topic has the right mindshare and shows encouraging results in many fields. With its inherent capability and the right amount of investment, this technology can contribute positively to the betterment of society across various sectors.

References and Resources

References and resources for further study and experimentation mentioned in alphabetical order.

- **Azure ML Studio**: https://studio.azureml.net/– Azure Machine Learning Studio is a GUI based integrated development environment for constructing and operationalizing machine learning workflow on Azure.

- **FFmpeg**: https://www.ffmpeg.org/– FFmpeg is a free software suite of libraries and programs for handling video, audio and other multimedia files and streams.

- **MNIST**: http://yann.lecun.com/exdb/mnist/– The MNIST is a large database of handwritten digits that is commonly used for training various image processing systems.

- **Natural Language Toolkit** (NLTK): https://www.nltk.org/– Natural Language Toolkit is a leading platform for building Python programs to work with natural language. NLTK provides a suite of processing libraries for tokenization, lemmatizing and parts of speech tagging of natural language text.

- **OpenCV** (Open Source Computer Vision Library): https://opencv.org/– OpenCV is an open source computer vision and machine learning library. OpenCV library has more than 2500 optimized algorithms to detect faces, identify objects and track moving objects.

- **Scikit-Learn:** http://scikit-learn.org – Scikit-learn is a free software machine learning library for the Python programming language. Provides simple and efficient tools for data mining and data analysis. It features various statistical machine learning techniques for regression, classification and clustering.

- **TensorFlow:** www.tensorflow.org – An open source machine learning library originally developed by researchers and engineers from Google. It comes with strong support for machine learning and deep learning across domains.